James Coventry,
Gentleman Photographer

Villages, Hamlets and Country Houses in the Fordingbridge / Ringwood Area

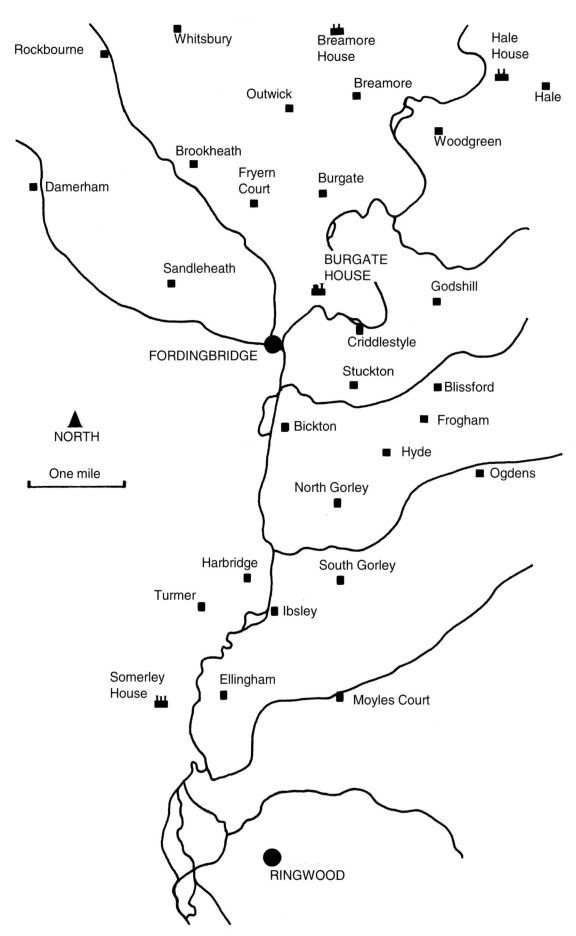

Other maps, covering the lower Avon valley and those parts of Dorset, Wiltshire, south-east Hampshire and Sussex which were visited by James Coventry, may be found on pages 88 and 89.

James Coventry, Gentleman Photographer

by Anthony Light and Gerald Ponting

Charlewood Press

Published by Charlewood Press
Middle Burgate House
Fordingbridge
SP6 1LX

http://home.clara.net/gponting/index-page10.html

British Library
Cataloguing in Publication Data
A catalogue record for this book is
available from the British Library

ISBN 0 95123 10 9 X

Typesetting, layout and design
by the authors using :
Microsoft Works 4,
Microsoft Word 97,
Corel PhotoPaint 8
and Serif PagePlus 5

Printed by Hobbs the Printers
Totton, Hants

Contents

Front cover photographs :
Ridley Wood, James Coventry, young nanny and thatched
cottage (see detailed captions on pages 45, 6 and 39
respectively).

James Seton Coventry, standing by a hatch in the Avon Valley near Burgate House.

This photograph, the only one known of James, was taken in the summer of 1893, when he was 44 years old.

It seems likely that the picture was taken by James's sister-in-law Emily, wife of his elder brother John, as she appears in the next consecutively numbered negative. This second photograph, which appears on page 23, was clearly taken nearby, and probably on the same day. However, there is little doubt that James would have set up the shot, just leaving Emily to operate the shutter. (Negative 780)

Authors' Preface

We first became 'acquainted' with James Coventry while working on an earlier book, *Fordingbridge and District - a Pictorial History*, which required the collection of a large number of old photographs. Among those people generously loaning prints was Mrs Allison of Frogham, whose late husband Phillip had had an extensive collection, including a number of superb photographs by James Coventry. We used twenty-nine of these pictures in the book, which was published by Phillimore in 1994.

Allison's prints had been made from the original quarter-plate glass negatives, of which around 270 are preserved in the Hampshire Record Office at Winchester. On examination of these negatives in the archives, it immediately became clear that James had been a very skilled photographer, both technically and artistically. Almost all of the negatives were in a good state of preservation, despite being about one hundred years old, so were capable of having modern prints produced from them.

The area covered by the photographs included not only Coventry's home area around Fordingbridge and the New Forest, but also extended out of Hampshire to Dorset, Wiltshire, Sussex and the Isle of Wight.

We soon began to think of producing a book based entirely on James's photography. The staff of the Record Office were supportive of the project and arranged to supply us with the modern prints which we needed.

While this went ahead, we produced a second book on Fordingbridge, concentrating on the Victorian period (*Victorian Journal - Fordingbridge 1837-1901*). While researching material for this book, we were loaned an album from the John Shering Collection which contained earlier photographic prints of the Coventry family.

Although the quality and standard of preservation of these 'snapshots' was much poorer than the pictures from the Record Office, they appeared to date from an earlier period, probably mainly the 1870s and 1880s. It seems more than probable that James was the photographer in this case also; and these pictures have proved a useful supplement to the more artistic later prints.

We managed to contact several members of the present-day Coventry family but were unable to glean much new information concerning James or his relations. In due course, however, we met James's niece, Mrs Gertrude Bower, then aged 95. Her wealth of family knowledge proved invaluable in supplementing our existing records, and in identifying the subjects of some of the photographs.

All of the photographs have been prepared for publication using appropriate computer software. The only manipulation carried out has been the removal of flaws caused by dust or scratches on the original negatives and the cropping of over-large areas of foreground or sky.

Apart from these improvements, you the reader are seeing the photographs just as their author first saw them around one hundred years ago. We hope that this collection of James Coventry's photographs will give you as much pleasure as it has given us to bring them to publication.

See a second view of this farmstead, with caption, on page 35. (Negative 2230)

7

James Coventry and his family

James Seton Coventry was born at Tywardreath in Cornwall in February 1849. He was the fourth child – and the second eldest son – in a family of twelve children. To set his life in context, we need to look a few generations further back.

The Coventry family had held estates at Burgate near Fordingbridge in Hampshire since the middle of the eighteenth century; and prior to this, the Bulkeley family had been at Burgate since Tudor times. It seems probable that a new manor-house was built by John Bulkeley Coventry-Bulkeley (youngest son of William, 5th Earl of Coventry) in about 1770. The surrounding Park was enclosed shortly afterwards.

On Coventry-Bulkeley's death in 1801, the estate passed to his nephew, John Coventry (son of George William, 6th Earl of Coventry), who was James's great-grandfather. It is believed that Burgate House was destroyed by fire and replaced in 1811 by the building which survives, largely unaltered, today (photograph below and page 17).

(A Coventry family tree appears on page 90.)

John Coventry (1793-1870; James's grandfather)

John's eldest son, also John, inherited the estate in 1829. In 1818, he had married Elizabeth Wilson of Corbridge, Northumberland; their eldest son, another John (James Coventry's father) had been born over the Scottish border at Roxburgh in 1819. It is clear that the family frequently lived away from their Burgate estates; certainly, from 1836 onwards, the House was leased to a succession of tenants who occupied it for the following quarter of a century. Even during these years of absence, however, there must have been occasional visits to Fordingbridge, in order to oversee the running of the estate.

Having left Burgate, John and Elizabeth moved to a small mansion called Plas Gwynant near Beddgelert on the southern edge of Snowdonia.

There can be little doubt that, like so many others, they had at some stage previously visited the area and fallen in love with its wild and beautiful scenery. Here they remained until the summer of 1850; their whereabouts in the following years is uncertain. After Elizabeth's death in 1856, John is known to have lived at St. John's Wood in Middlesex and then at Moortown House, Ringwood.

John re-married very quickly and was rapidly widowed again, his second wife, Louisa, dying in 1857. Now in his late 60s, he returned to Burgate in 1860 with his third wife, Ellen Wyndham (née Penruddock). He died there eleven years later but his widow, much his junior, outlived him by more than thirty years.

John Coventry (1819-1897; James's father)

In all probability, it was on one of the family's visits back to Fordingbridge that John and Elizabeth's eldest son met Catherine Seton of Brookheath. They were married in the parish church at Fordingbridge on 21st June 1842. (The Setons were an ancient Scottish family; Catherine's grandfather had been Governor of the island of St Vincent in the Caribbean. Her brother, James Seton, achieved the unenviable distinction, in 1845, of becoming the last person to die as the result of a duel on English soil.)

The young couple moved to Cornwall so that John could pursue his chosen career in the church. Following family tradition he had obtained his qualifications at Oxford University, having been admitted to Magdalen Hall on 12th October 1838, at the age of 19. He was awarded his B.A. degree there in 1842, the year of his marriage.

In the following year, John and Catherine's first child was born at Fowey, where John was Curate. However, his determination to complete his education saw the family move back to Oxford, this time to the nearby village of Iffley. He was again admitted to Magdalen Hall, where he gained his Master of Arts degree in 1845.

Back in Cornwall, John had a short spell as rector of Tywardreath near St Austell. It was here, on 18th March 1849, that his fourth child, James Seton Coventry, was christened, taking his mother's maiden name as his middle name. James's christening was recorded in the family bible with the entry shown below.

Although, at the age of 22, James was eventually to settle at Burgate, it seems unlikely that he knew it well in his childhood, if at all. His early years must have been spent in a succession of church houses, as his parents moved from parish to parish.

A fifth child was born at Milford in Surrey, while the next four were all born in Devon. On 9th March 1852, John was appointed as Assistant Curate of St. Michael's, West Hill, Ottery St. Mary at an annual stipend of £40.

4th James Seton born 26th Feby 1849 & christened 18th March at Tywardreath Cornwall. —

The Coventrys' Conversion to the Roman Catholic Church

Increasingly John was influenced by the Oxford Movement within the Church of England, known to its supporters as the Catholic Revival. John Henry Newman, one of the leaders of the movement, transferred his allegiance to Rome, becoming a Catholic in 1845. His 'defection' was widely publicised and many other Church of England clergymen reconsidered their positions as a result.

John Coventry, with his wife and nine children, was received into the Catholic Church in 1857. His father, a staunch Protestant, was outraged. Ostracised by family and friends, John and Catherine decided to move abroad, settling at la Vallinière pres Vouvray, near Tours in France. Here, with a like-minded community of English colleagues and under the influence of the Servite Fathers, they were able to practice Catholicism free from the prejudices prevalent in the England of the day.

Having given up the income from his church living and with no support from his father, John was now almost entirely dependent upon his wife's family fortune. Life was hard and the material advantages normally resulting from their position in society were largely lacking. Three more children were born to them here between 1859 and 1863.

It was in these circumstances that James and his brothers and sisters spent their childhoods. Catholicism dominated their lives, especially as their father undertook the education of James, his elder brother John and his next younger brother Walter (and perhaps others in the family as well). The intensity of their convictions is exemplified by James's decision to become a Pontifical Zouave at the age of 19; and by the fact that, as we shall see later, one of his brothers joined the Catholic priesthood and three of his sisters became nuns.

The family's departure from France, at the time of the Franco-Prussian war, was a dramatic one. The following story was told by James's sister Gertrude, who was nine years old at the time of the event described (passed on to us by her daughter, Gertrude Bower) :

> The invading Prussian armies gained the upper hand on the armies of Napoleon III's Second Empire and inflicted a crushing defeat at the battle of Sedan on 1st September 1870. On that same day, some of the Coventry children had had a bonfire in their garden at la Vallinière. Local people wrote 'mort aux Anglais' on their gates, assuming that the English family was celebrating the Prussian victory. The family departed in haste and secrecy during the night, leaving most of their belongings behind, and passing through Paris the day before it was besieged. They then lived on the outskirts of London for a spell, before moving to Bournemouth.

(The surrender at Sedan having taken place on 1st September, the siege of Paris began on the 19th.)

The Death of James's Grandfather

At Bournemouth the family joined with others in promoting the construction of a new Catholic church, but their stay there was curtailed by the serious illness of James's grandfather, John senior, at Burgate House. The earlier bitterness over his son's conversion remained and, even as he lay dying, John refused to allow his son and heir, John junior, to see him. It is said that, had it been legally possible, he would certainly have withheld his inheritance. Being bound by the terms of his own father's will, however, he could do nothing to alter the descent of either Burgate House or the Estates.

His personal possessions were a different matter. The contents of the House were left almost in their entirety to his wife Wyndham, while £6000 was set aside for the benefit of his remaining children. John junior was mentioned only once in his will. Four silver side bowls with the Coventry Crest were to be held in trust by Wyndham, for the use of John junior during his lifetime.

Wyndham had no use for the furniture and other effects, so decided to have a sale, conducted by Hannen's, the local auctioneers. It lasted for three days and included every single item remaining, both from within the House and from the gardens, yards and stables. John junior, who would otherwise have been left with an empty house, was forced to buy back much of the furniture and effects, at considerable personal cost.

Having died on 13th October 1871 at the age of 78 years, John senior was buried a week later in the family vault in the nave of Fordingbridge parish church (seen in the photograph below - neg. 1683).

The terms of his will had stated that his remains were

> to be deposited in the nearest Burial Ground of the Church of England where I may be residing at the time of my decease - My funeral to be quiet and unostentatious and to be conducted as economically as possible consistent with the feelings of those I leave behind me.

His family and about fifty of his tenants attended the church service and he was buried in a handsome oak coffin with an inscribed silver plate. 'Quiet' and 'unostentatious' are relative terms!

Burgate House and Estate, 1870s

Burgate House now became a hive of activity as John, his wife and their twelve children, ranging in age from eight to twenty-eight, settled in. Several of them, including James, were destined to stay there for many years, although others gradually moved away to begin the next stage of their lives. Walter joined the Public Works Department in Cape Town; Alexander Moray joined the Servite Order at Bognor Regis as their first English novice; and Bernard was appointed as an agricultural advisor to the Indian government. Marion, Isabella and Barbara became nuns. Surprisingly, only four of the twelve children married.

The day-to-day running of the Estate must have occupied a great deal of John's time. On the basis of family papers and the memories of others, one of John's grand-daughters described him as *'a Holy, generous and amusing man, a great raconteur, but with no business acumen'*. However, much of the burden of estate affairs was no doubt lifted from his shoulders, thanks to the help and advice of his Steward, Mr John Hannen, the experienced local Estate Agent and Auctioneer.

The Building of Fordingbridge Catholic Church

The promotion of Catholicism was still John's overriding priority. One of his first acts was to plan a private Oratory in Burgate House with a priest to say masses, something which would have horrified his father! It was also John's dream to establish a Catholic community in Fordingbridge. To this end he gave the Servite Fathers, all Italians, a sum of £1000 and two acres of land from his estate, together with an endowment of £100 a year. The intention was to build a small monastic house and church. Work began in 1872 on the old cricket pitch, just to the north of the town, at Calves Close.

The late Muriel Coventry, in her notes on local Catholicism, revealed that problems soon arose.

> *Unfortunately instead of (John) seeing the project through himself by his chosen architect it was left to the Fathers - all Italians with large ideas with what they could do with the money. The present church was intended to be the refectory and at that stage building had to stop.*

In fact, Fordingbridge Catholic Church, as it stands today, was intended to be a refectory, with a dormitory above; the intervening floor was removed when it was discovered that insufficient cash remained to build a church as well!

Once the adapted church was open for worship by local Catholics, there was further controversy. John's endowment to the Servites had made additional provision for the resident priest *'to say two masses per week in the private Oratory of Mr Coventry'*. According to the regulations of the Catholic Church, John was the 'Primary Indult' in this arrangement – he was the person allowed a specific deviation from the Church's common law. The rules did not allow masses to be said for the family when John himself was absent. As a result,

> *Mr Coventry without taking notice of the church laws, refused to pay the donations and implicitly threatened a law suit in a secular court if they would not say Mass in his Oratory even in his absence. So the Holy See … benignly granted to extend the privilege of Primary Indult to three other individuals of his family. But not even with this did he declare himself content …*

No doubt due to this dispute, the Servite Fathers left Fordingbridge in 1875 and did not return till 1888. In the meantime there was a succession of priests, presumably co-operating with John Coventry's demands.

Photographs of the exterior and interior of the Catholic Church of Our Lady of Seven Dolours, Fordingbridge. These - and all other photographs which are enclosed in boxes - are taken from Coventry family albums.

John Coventry (1845-1933; James's elder brother)

On 25th October 1876, James's brother John, the heir to the estates, married Emily Weld of Lymington. The Welds were a leading Catholic family whose main seat is, today, still at Lulworth in Dorset. The wedding took place at Lymington but 'a sumptuous dinner was provided for the tenants of the estate at the Crown Hotel (in Fordingbridge), which was presided over by Mr Hannen, the steward of the manor'.

On John and Emily's return to Fordingbridge after their wedding tour, there were elaborate festivities in the town, as recorded by the *Salisbury and Winchester Journal* :

> On Wednesday, this town was a scene of animation on the arrival of Mr. John Coventry and his wife from their wedding tour. A procession was formed in the Market-place, and 60 men were supplied with torches, and proceeded to the Railway Station, headed by the South Hants Band, and followed by a number of Odd Fellows and Foresters, together with many of the tenantry. The station was prettily decorated. On the arrival of Mr. and Mrs. Coventry they were received by Mr. Hannen, the steward of the manor, and proceeded to their carriage. The procession then left the station, the torches being lighted and coloured fires displayed at intervals. At the entrance to Burgate Park, there was a gas illumination, and a triumphal arch of evergreens, &c., had been erected, and the avenue to the house was illuminated on each side with variegated lamps.

An address of congratulation was read on behalf of the tradesmen. A number of presentations were made on behalf of the tenant farmers and of 'the 65 most humble and lowly tenants of the estate'.

> During the reading of the address, some of Brock's celebrated Crystal Palace fires were lit. Rockets were fired as a signal for parting, and the band led the way from the Park to the town, playing 'God Save the Queen'. It is computed that over 2000 persons were present. The town was gaily decorated for the occasion.

As a married man John soon sought a career. His interest in estate management led to him taking over the day-to-day running of the Burgate Estate from his less-than-enthusiastic father. Before long his ambitions led him elsewhere, however, as he took up an appointment as Land Agent to another staunch Catholic, Sir Percy Radcliffe of Rudding Park in Yorkshire. (Gertrude, the youngest of John and James's sisters, was to marry Percy's son, Henry, in 1896.)

Much of John's time was now spent at the estate office at Draycott, near Stoke on Trent, with occasional visits to London and north to Tadcaster. There were, however, periodic trips south to visit family members in Fordingbridge, Lymington and Lulworth.

(See photograph of John and Emily on page 19.)

James Coventry – photography and estate management

With John busy in the north, the administrative responsibilities for the Burgate Estate fell to James, assisted by frequent and detailed correspondence with his elder brother. By this time, the financial situation at Burgate was far from satisfactory. The pressures of having inherited a large estate, without the considerable capital necessary to back it up, were beginning to tell. The position was exacerbated by the agricultural depression of the time which considerably reduced rental incomes. Funds could be raised only by mortgaging or selling some of the property. From the mid-1880s, selected lands and houses were offered for sale, resulting in a gradual, but significant, reduction in the size of the Estates.

It was in this climate that James's interest in the relatively expensive hobby of photography had grown up, certainly by 1882, perhaps much earlier. Many of the amateur photographers of this time, and particularly of earlier decades, were members of the gentry and aristocracy. Few other people had the leisure time or the finance to indulge in the new hobby – or indeed the space required to set up a darkroom.

Clearly the time expended in taking and developing a large number of plates was considerable and how this fitted in with his estate work can only be guessed at. Which took priority is unclear, but family tradition seems to be that he was not a particularly good estate manager. Certainly there are more than a few letters in the archives, in which Mr Hannen was giving James frequent reminders to answer letters or pay bills. He did not, in any case, have the authority to take important decisions without reference to his elder brother. As an example of this brotherly advice, John wrote to him while staying in a house party at Lulworth Castle :

> I will write again to Hannen, when I get back, about the agreements – I never thought the tenants would pay for the Stamps – It is usual for the landlord to do them – and the tenant gets a copy which he can get stamped if he likes – but never does. It is just one of those cases where you may go on for years without ever having to bother or requiring to produce an agreement, and then something may turn up which may cause no end of bother & expense because they are not in proper form.

In 1880, one of his younger brothers, Bernard, wrote from Ceylon while on a passage to India :

> … writing to you to wish you many happy returns of your birthday. I enclose as a present what is called a tobacco pouch here but leave you to judge its merits in that respect.
> I hope that you are getting on well with the farm. If we were to get such fine weather as we have here I think farming would pay in England. The thermometer is above 80° in the shade and the barometer is above 31 in. and this they call the winter season.

Here James has photographed two members of his family at the King and Queen Oaks at Bolderwood in the New Forest. His sister Isabella Coventry (known to the family as Ella), who was five years younger than James, eventually became a nun. His brother Bernard, ten years his junior, later worked in agricultural research in India. The King and Queen Oaks, believed to be so-called simply because of their size, were much visited in Victorian times, but today exist only as rotting stumps. (1403)

The brother to whom James seems to have been closest was Walter Bulkeley Coventry, his junior by just one year. A series of letters dated 1882 and 1883 describe his life when he was settling into a job in the Public Works Department in Cape Town. Photography is mentioned twice in Walter's letters, showing his awareness of James's interest in the topic. In July 1882 :

> I have had my photograph taken here … It is a horrible production but I send you one as a specimen of south African photography …

and in August :

> I am glad to hear that the 'Lord Lieutenant' has been photographed successfully and I shall be delighted to have one of his portraits.

This seems to suggest that James took on casual 'commissions' from time to time, an idea supported by an intriguingly naïve letter from a friend at Lyndhurst, received on 16th May 1896 :

> Park Cottage, Lyndhurst
> Dear Mr James
> I am writing to ask you if you got your coat quite safe I sent it by post so I expect you did only you have been to busy to write.
> I am going to ask you a favour do you think you could do one of my Photos in my ball dress for me soon because I have promised one to someone who is going away they are going the end of next week so I am afraid you will not have time but if you have will you try and do me one. I do not know whether we shall come for Whit Tuesday or not but I hope we shall Charlie is longing to have one of his Photos too but you will do me one of mine if you can wont you or two if you like when are you coming again not this summer I expect
> now I must say
> Good Bye From Puppsy
> Write soon

At least two of James's photographs were published as picture postcards – one of the bridge at Fordingbridge (page 29) and one of a cottage near Hyde Common (page 41). We have no evidence to show whether this was done on a commercial basis or whether more than these two were available in this format.

The Sale of the Burgate Estates

The death of James's father in November 1897 precipitated a major crisis in the family. James and his fellow-Trustees, appointed a few years previously, were charged with selling the entire property after John's decease. This was necessary to pay off mortgages and other charges, which were a considerable and constant drain on the estate. These charges included annual payments from the sum of £6000 set aside by James's grandfather in 1871.

As a result, the centuries-old possessions of the Manor of Burgate were dispersed irrevocably. The bulk of the sale – 1680 acres of land with numerous houses and cottages valued at a total annual rental income of nearly £3,000 – took place in 1898. Some of the land was purchased by developers, resulting in the building of streets of Victorian villas to the north of Fordingbridge Catholic Church. The remainder of the outlying properties were sold in the following year.

A more serious matter to the family was the potential loss of Burgate House itself. This, too, had to be auctioned. Much to his relief, John was able to buy back both the House and the adjoining Park at the sale held at the White Hart in Salisbury on 8th August.

By the middle of 1900, the estate was gone and the legal process was virtually complete. The dismay of the family was exacerbated by a row over the future of the House. Having bought it, John now intended to return there with his wife and six children. His mother, Catherine, would be provided, in the customary way, with a dower house nearby. His brothers and sisters objected vehemently to this and argued that she should be allowed to spend the rest of her days at Burgate.

John's views prevailed, however. Catherine moved to the house called *The Bartons*, where she died less than two years later. In her will, proved on 17th June 1901, she left her house to James and Walter and the majority of her remaining possessions to her other children. John, her eldest son, was left nothing, on the grounds that he was *'already well provided for'*.

James's departure from Burgate House

Most of James's brothers and sisters had by now left Burgate – four were married, three were settled in nunneries, some were working abroad. James, having taken his mother's side in the dispute over the House, could hardly expect to remain there and to share it with his brother John and family.

He was left with little option, at the age of 51, but to find a new home. When making his will in 1909 he was apparently at a house in Fordingbridge called *The Warren*, but Gertrude Bower remembers him staying with the Lonnen family at Parsonage Farm. As a young girl she was sometimes taken with her brother to visit her elderly bachelor 'Uncle Jimmy'. She remembers thinking of him as *'a funny old thing, a hypochondriac; his rooms always filled with all sorts of medicines'*. She does not remember him then having any active interest in photography.

James ended his days in an apartment belonging to a Mr George Oates at *Fermaine* in Station Road, Fordingbridge. He died there on April 12th 1917 and was laid to rest next to his parents in the graveyard of the Catholic Church at Fordingbridge. Under the terms of his short and simple will he left to his brother Walter Bulkeley Coventry *'all that I die possessed of and may become entitled to after my death'*.

There can be little doubt that in his later years he had become a rather sad and lonely bachelor living on the memories of happier times, perhaps looking back on his albums of photographs (most of which are now sadly lost). Probably, he regarded his acceptance as 'a Pontifical Zouave' to be the highlight of his life. Certainly, his family thought so, as these were the words chosen as the inscription for his memorial stone. (See next page.)

Subsequent Coventry family history

James's brother John remained at Burgate House until his death in 1933; his widow, Emily, occupied it till her death in 1939. This ended a Bulkeley-Coventry occupation which had lasted since 1446. The house was occupied by ICI for a while and is now (designated 'Burgate Manor') the national headquarters of The Game Conservancy Trust.

Two of Bernard's daughters, Muriel and Isabella, (James's nieces) lived for many years at Frogham. They are well-remembered by many people living around the Fordingbridge area today as 'the two Miss Coventrys'. Muriel wrote some notes on the family history which have proved very useful to us.

There are only a few members of the Coventry family, descended in the male line from John and Elizabeth who married in 1818, living today. Although there were large families in several generations, many members of the family became nuns or priests or otherwise never married. John and Emily's son, John Joseph Coventry (the fifth eldest son in succession to be called John) had five daughters but no sons.

These portraits of John Joseph Coventry and of his wife Margaret Camilla (née Macartney), who married in 1910, were painted in 1914 by C. Macartney. The original oil paintings are still at Burgate House today, in the possession of The Game Conservancy Trust.

James Coventry and the Zouaves

When James Coventry died in 1917, aged 68, the following was inscribed on his tombstone in the 'Coventry corner' of the Fordingbridge Catholic Churchyard :

IHS
Pray for the repose of the soul
of
James Seton Coventry
Pontifical Zouave
Born 26 February 1849
Died 12 April 1917
R.I.P.

It is intriguing to wonder why his service with the Pontifical Zouaves was the one aspect of his life which relatives considered worth recording on his tombstone.

Who were the Zouaves ?

Today, few people are even aware of the meaning of the term Zouave. Throughout much of the nineteenth century they were better known than the French Foreign Legion. The name originated from the *Zouaoua*, a fiercely independent tribe living in the hills of Algeria and Morocco. After the French conquest, groups of Zouaoua fighters were organised into two battalions of auxiliaries within the French Army.

While more and more native Frenchmen joined the Zouave units, they retained a distinctive and colourful North African uniform – a short, collar-less jacket over a sleeveless vest, baggy trousers tied with a long woollen sash, white canvas leggings and a tasselled fez and turban.

By 1852, the Zouaves were made up entirely of Frenchmen. Under Louis Napoleon, they were integrated into three regiments of the regular French Army. In the Crimean War of 1854-55 and in later battles for the control of northern Italy, their exploits became widely known.

U.S. Army Captain George B. McClellan, having seen Zouaves in action, praised them as *'The finest light infantry that Europe can produce … the beau-ideal of a soldier'*. Many considered them the epitome of bravery; they enjoyed a reputation of being reckless on the battlefield, as though warfare were merely a game, and their lives simply the table stakes. It was not long before militia units on both sides of the American Civil War began to adopt the North African uniform and to call themselves Zouaves.

The Pontifical Zouaves

In mid-nineteenth century Europe, all that remained of the Holy Roman Empire was a small area of central Italy, known as the Papal States, which had remained under the control of the Pope for eleven centuries. The Pontifical Zouaves were formed in 1861 to replace units of the French army which had previously protected the temporal sovereignty of the Pope. (It seems somewhat ironical that the head of the Catholic Church was protected by soldiers dressing in uniforms originating in Moslem North Africa!)

While they were recruited mainly from French soldiers already in Rome, young men of the Catholic faith from other parts of Europe, James Coventry included, were also keen to join.

A detachment of Pontifical Zouaves aided France during the Franco-Prussian War of 1870-71; but by this time, James had left the Zouaves. Following the unification of Italy, the Pontifical Zouaves were disbanded in 1871. Zouave units remained part of the French army, however, until 1915.

James Coventry's service with the Pontifical Zouaves

Tracking down the details of James's service with the Zouaves, as recorded in the 1920 publication *'Matricule des Zouaves Pontificaux : Liste des Zouaves'*, involved an Internet contact with the Bibliothèque Nationale du Québec in Montréal.

On page 202 of the second volume, this information is recorded about James Coventry :

7173   COVENTRY, JACQUES, né a Londres (Angleterre), 26 février 1849. – Z.P., 2 mars 1868. Libéré, 12 juillet 1868, ord m.

[COVENTRY, JAMES, born in London [sic] (England), 26th February 1849. – (Joined) the Pontifical Zouaves, 2nd March 1868. Discharged by ministerial order, 12th July 1868.]

This makes the inscription on his tomb even more intriguing – he was a member of the Pontifical Zouaves *for less than six months, at the age of nineteen*! Many of his contemporaries had equally short periods of service.

The Coventrys being a devout Catholic family, it is clear that they were all very proud of the fact that one of their number, however briefly, had been a member of the Pope's own elite troops. While James seems to have spent much of his working life helping to manage the family estate, and we remember him as a skilled photographer when in his forties and fifties, the family obviously took much more pride in the fact that he had been a 'Pontifical Zouave'.

Zouave uniforms - as worn by the Association des zouaves pontificaux de Trois-Rivières in 1931 - courtesy of the Archives nationales de Québec

James Coventry's Photography in Context

Photography 1827-1890s

It is generally accepted that the first photographs were taken by Joseph Nièpce in 1827. His method, however, was not a very practical proposition, exposure times being around eight hours in full sunlight!

Louis Daguerre introduced the 'Daguerreotype' in 1839 and many studios using this method were still operating two decades later. Ultimately, however, the daguerreotype proved to be a dead-end. The main reason was that each picture was unique; there was no easy way of producing more than a single copy of each image.

William Henry Fox Talbot, Lord of the Manor of Lacock in Wiltshire, introduced the negative-positive process which was to become the basis of photography as we know it today. His earliest paper negatives date from 1835.

In 1847, the glass-plate negative was introduced and four years later the wet collodion process. The glass plates were wet when used in the camera and required chemical treatment both immediately before and immediately after exposure. Thus any work away from the studio required a portable darkroom. The resulting pictures were often superbly sharp and detailed, but the laborious process largely precluded the development of amateur photography.

Dry plates first appeared in the 1870s; in the next decade, they came into general use. Professional or amateur photographers could now buy stocks of ready-to-use glass plates which could be processed whenever convenient.

Thus James Coventry, as an amateur photographer in the 1890s, benefited from the ready availability of convenient dry plates. He used plates measuring 4¼ x 3¼ inches which were known as 'quarter-plate'. A 'whole-plate' photograph measures 8½ x 6½ inches – a term which derives from the standard size of Victorian window glass!

Two hundred and seventy-four of his quarter-plate glass negatives still exist, preserved in the Hampshire Record Office. Each negative has a number scratched in the emulsion, presumably James's own consecutive numbering system. The highest number recorded is 5624, an indication of how prolific he must have been as a photographer.

The Lancaster Instantograph

Thanks to the preservation in the archives of a collection of the family's receipts and invoices, we know the details of some of James's photographic purchases. These were delivered by rail to Fordingbridge from two suppliers in London – Jonathan Fallowfield's Central Photographic Stores in Charing Cross Road and B. J. Edwards & Co. of Hackney.

On 16th August 1895, he purchased a new camera. (We do not know what he was using before this, except that it must have been a quarter-plate model.) Fallowfield's invoiced him for 'One ¼ Lancaster Special Brass Bound, Camera Slide', cost £2.10s.0d, together with '5 Extra Double DK Slides'

at nine shillings and six-pence each. The total bill, with a 5% cash discount, came to £4.12s.6d. The 'dark slides' were a necessary means of transporting the glass plate negatives and of transferring them to the camera without exposing them to the light.

J. Lancaster and Son were among the top camera manufacturers of the time, their Instantograph selling in tens of thousands. The quarter-plate was the smallest of several models – the nearest thing to a 'compact' camera of its day. Such constructions of mahogany, brass and leather are very collectable today; and Rob Niederman, an American antique camera enthusiast, comments :

> The camera was likely a fine choice. It is small and robust (the body and bed being made of thick mahogany). The folded body dimensions are: 14 cm wide x 15.3 cm high x 6.5 cm deep [approx. 5½ x 12 x 2½ inches]. The bed and body sides are respectively 1.4 cm and 0.8 cm thick [0.55 x 0.3 inches] – actually quite thick for such a small camera.

In use, the camera would normally have been mounted on a tripod. The front of the case would fold forwards to a horizontal position and the lens would slide out, connected to the main body by a leather bellows. (See contemporary advertisement above.)

There was no viewfinder, the photographer composing his picture upside down on a full-size ground-glass screen. To see this clearly, a cloth would be placed over head and camera. Rotating the lens barrel changed the aperture; turning knurled brass knobs caused the lens to rack backwards and forwards on rails, thus bringing the picture into focus. When all was ready, the 'dark-slide' containing the plate would be fitted to the back of the camera and a panel slid upwards, so that the glass surface was facing the lens.

The 'Instantograph Shutter', used to make the exposure, was a relatively new development on James's model. On many earlier cameras of a similar type, the mechanical shutter was an optional extra, fitted on the front of the lens. (In cameras with no shutter, exposure was effected by removing and replacing the lens cap!)

The panel would then be slid back so that the dark slide could be removed from the camera without exposing the negative to the light.

The dark slide could later be replaced in the camera, the opposite way round, for a second plate to be exposed. The number of photographs which could be taken between visits to the darkroom would depend upon the number of dark slides carried. Six dark slides, each containing two glass plates, would have been somewhat bulkier than the folded camera.

Plates, papers and chemicals

The archives contain a particularly large number of invoices from 1894; in that year James purchased at least 19 dozen plates, providing 228 exposures. He normally ordered his plates in batches of three dozen at a cost of five shillings and three-pence. In terms of exposures, this is exactly equivalent to a modern 36-exposure film! The cost translates to around 26p in decimal currency; more meaningful is the calculation that it would have bought the equivalent of twenty large loaves.

Other purchases in 1894 included a box to hold 100 quarter-plate negatives, 100 8x6 Cream Mounts, four albums, mountant, and ten packets of Printing Out Paper. It is clear that James Coventry did his own processing from the purchase of various chemicals including '½ lb. Sulp. Soda, 1 lb. Chrome Alum, 7 lbs. Hypo, 1 oz. Pyro' at a grand total of two shillings and ninepence. While most of these chemicals were standard for the time, pyrogallol was an interesting choice for a negative developer. It is a surface developer, producing a particularly sharp image; its disadvantages are that it is unstable and stains the skin. James Coventry may well have had permanently darkened fingertips!

In the same collection of invoices, there is a postcard dated 1893, reminding James to renew his subscription to *Amateur Photographer*, the long-established magazine which is still on weekly sale today.

Dating the Photographs

None of the surviving negatives are dated, although they were numbered by James, apparently in chronological order. Thus the earliest we have is no. 34 and the latest no. 5624. (These numbers are given in brackets at the end of each relevant caption.)

A few pictures can be dated fairly precisely from their content, for example, the great Avon Valley floods of November 1894 and celebrations for the Coronation of Edward VII in August 1902. By using these as starting points, it is possible to establish an overall framework into which most

shots can be fitted satisfactorily. In addition, by examining the background foliage where relevant, it is usually easy to determine whether a photograph was taken in summer or in winter.

Using this scheme it would seem likely that James began using quarter-plate glass negatives in 1891 at the very latest, although we know that he had begun his photography at an earlier date. The end date is harder to determine, but would seem to be 1905, or possibly rather later if he was taking pictures less frequently in his later years.

James Coventry's Photographic Style and Subjects

We have no idea who edited James's negatives down to the 274 which remain today. He may have edited them himself in later life or this may have been done by some other member of the family, perhaps long before the collection was deposited in the Hampshire Record Office in 1984.

The remaining negatives are almost all technically superb; although, with 95% of James's known work apparently having been destroyed, we have no means of knowing how many over-exposed or under-exposed negatives there may have been originally. Maybe some had deteriorated over time; certainly even a few of those in the HRO collection are now unusable due to the emulsion becoming detached from the glass.

Another result of the editing of the collection is that we have no means of knowing if the remaining negatives accurately reflect the type of photography which interested him most. However, a rough analysis of the subjects is of interest. Inevitably, there is some overlap in categories in this analysis.

landscapes	85
trees	48
town and village scenes	43
churches and cathedrals	27
country houses	23
family	20
cottages	15
coastal	13

The most striking aspect of this is the large proportion of photographs best described as 'tree portraits', of which those on page 45 of this book are representative. Most of these were taken in the New Forest, including a sequence of about 25 consecutive negatives taken in the winter of 1894-95 in Vereley Wood, Burley. Even allowing for the editing process, it is obvious that James had a great interest in trees!

Many of James's landscapes feature rivers, streams, ponds, even flooding of the Avon valley near his Burgate home. But perhaps the most notable features of James's photographs are the children who appear in them. His niece, Gertrude Bower, told us that 'Uncle Jimmy was mad on taking children, school feasts, and so on'. Most of the young girls who appear in so many of his landscapes and village scenes were no doubt his nieces or other members of his extended family.

Artistically, we consider James to have been a brilliant photographer – our motive in producing this book has been to introduce his work to a much wider public.

Burgate House and the Coventry Family

Burgate House, on the outskirts of Fordingbridge, was the home of the Coventry family from the eighteenth century. The existing house dates from 1811 and is a fine, unspoilt example of Regency 'Gothick'.

The Burgate Estates were sold off in 1897 but the house remained in possession of the Coventry family till 1939. Today it goes by the name of 'Burgate Manor' and, with modern rear extensions, is the headquarters of The Game Conservancy Trust.

Inevitably, James Coventry took many photographs of the house and of its grounds. This view from the south-west (above), probably taken in the summer of 1896, shows James's elder brother John and wife Emily. The large stone 'balls' near the front entrance are still a feature of the much wider drive today. (1405)

ABOVE : One of the Coventry girls admiring the flowers in the greenhouse. It was attached to the eastern side of Burgate House (as seen in the main picture). An archway of peach trees is under-planted with a wide variety of chrysanthemums. (1951)

RIGHT : The South Lodge of Burgate Park gave access direct to Fordingbridge town, while the North Lodge stood at the gateway leading towards Burgate village and Salisbury.

Both lodges survive, but much of the former park is now occupied by modern housing. The North Lodge, seen here, still has its thatched roof today, but stands adjacent to the northern end of the Fordingbridge by-pass. (1505)

LEFT : Three early pictures from the Coventry photograph album in the John Shering Collection. In this album, they are captioned, respectively :

'Old Mare and Penney'
'Flo'
'Pepper'

No doubt, Flo and Pepper, who appear together in another snapshot in the album, were very pampered pets!

Penney also appears in the guise of a coachman in another photograph, on page 62. However, there is no record of a Mr Penney in either the 1881 or 1891 census records for Fordingbridge.

BELOW : This is the main entrance to Burgate House, with Emily Coventry sitting in the donkey cart and James's sister Gertrude, thirteen years his junior, standing by the donkey.

Gertrude later married Henry Radcliffe, another keen photographer. (Their daughter, Mrs Gertrude Bower, was able to assist us in the identification of many of the family photographs.) The donkey is probably Mouly, successor to Robin who appeared in some earlier pictures. Both donkeys were frequently used by Gertrude, who grew very attached to them. (133)

This group photograph was almost certainly taken in the grounds of Burgate House in May 1897. The so-called 'leg-of-mutton' blouse sleeves, tightly fitting, but puffed at the shoulder, were fashionable only in the second half of the 1890s. The seated figures are Emily Coventry and her husband John, James's elder brother. The group of young men and women standing behind them may include John and Emily's three eldest daughters who were around 20, 18 and 17 at the time. The others are presumably friends or more distant members of the family.

Only a few months after this photograph was taken, John and James's father died. This resulted in the break-up of the Burgate Estates, though John was able to buy back Burgate House and its surrounding park. (See page 12.) (1710)

In addition to the Coventry family photograph album which is in the John Shering Collection, there were a number of others, whose present whereabouts we have been unable to discover. Some pictures from them were copied by Phillip Allison in the 1970s. His copy prints, including the two shown below, are also held by the HRO, separately from the main James Coventry collection.

Philomena Coventry, one of James's nieces, holding the reins of the donkey in a farmyard with a small staddle-stone barn in the background. The boy on the donkey is likely to be her younger brother William, who would have been six years old in the summer of 1899. William was destined to be killed in action in 1914, while Mena took up a vocation as a nun. (PA 5/26)

Unidentified girl with a man's bicycle, standing by a haystack. The bicycle may well be the same one which appears in the picture on page 43. (PA 6/76)

Three of the younger members of the Coventry family in fancy dress. The dark-haired girl in the centre is probably Philomena. The younger girl on the left, dressed as Annie Oakley, the famous 1890s Wild West sharp-shooter, may be their younger sister Annette. In later life, Annette married Major-General Sir Philip Grant. Their son became a Rear Admiral. (1609)

John Joseph (Jack) Coventry, at the age of about 14, wearing a clown costume decorated with cats and rabbits. He had been born at Burgate in 1882; as eldest son, he took charge of the remains of the estate after the death of his father, in 1933. Following the death of his mother, Emily, six years later, he sold Burgate House to ICI. Portraits of Jack and of his wife Margaret are seen on page 13. (1614)

The young lady reading a book at one of the windows along the south front of Burgate House is believed to be Mary Flora Coventry, known to the family as May. She was born in 1877, the eldest of John and Emily's seven children; she remained unmarried. Note the birdcage in the background. (1500)

A group of young girls, presumably mostly members of the Coventry family, playing 'Aunt Sally' on the lawn at Burgate Cottage, later Burgate Court. The wooden 'Aunt Sally' figure has a net to catch any balls thrown through her open mouth. (1673)

This picture was almost certainly taken later that same afternoon, when the group had doubled in size. They now appear to be playing 'Ring-a-ring o' Roses'. The front of the 'Aunt Sally' can be seen in the background. (1674)

This delightfully rustic wooden footbridge crossed a stream which runs into the River Avon near Burgate House. In the foreground are the neat lawns and shrubberies of the grounds; on the other side of the bridge are willow trees in the meadows. Roofs of some houses in the town of Fordingbridge can just be seen through the distant trees on the left. (2523)

Three more snapshots from the family album :

ABOVE LEFT : 'Down the River' - a view from the lawns of Burgate House, looking south down the River Avon.

ABOVE RIGHT : 'Cow Bridge, Burgate' - another rustic bridge, used for cows from a neighbouring farm to reach grazing in the water meadows. A footbridge on the same site today is a mini-suspension-bridge and forms part of the Avon Valley Path from Salisbury to Christchurch.

LEFT : 'Boathouse, Burgate' - several of James's photographs, including two of those opposite, show members of the family enjoying boating on the river. This is the family's thatched boathouse.

Two more of Phillip Allison's copies from the missing albums.

'Aunt E and girls' - this is undoubtedly Emily Coventry (née Weld), James's sister-in-law. The girls in the rowing boat with her are probably her three eldest daughters, Mary, Constance and Philomena, then aged about 16, 14 and 13. The photograph was taken shortly after the portrait of James Coventry himself which appears on page 6. In both pictures, houses on the Fordingbridge - Godshill road can be distinguished. (PA 6/77)

An uncaptioned snapshot, of rather poor quality, but included for the obvious enjoyment of the three girls, clearly quite used to 'mucking about in boats'! (PA 6/75)

The photograph below is typical of James Coventry's work – a rural scene featuring trees, water and children in a well-balanced composition. The wooden structure is one of the many hatches which were used, up until the mid-twentieth century, to control the irrigation of the water meadows at Burgate and throughout much of the Avon valley.

These two girls, carefully posed by the hatch, may well be James's nieces, Philomena and Annette, who also appear in the fancy dress picture. They would have been 19 and 15 respectively when the photograph was taken in the summer of 1899. At first sight, the girls in the picture look younger than this, but it is difficult to judge ages when the fashions are so different from those of today. (2517)

Friends of the Family

The family album in the Shering Collection contains not only photographs of the family and of the Burgate estate but also shots of other country houses round-about and various friends of the Coventry family.

Prominent among the friends are the Foleys of Packham House, Fordingbridge; the Heathcotes of Merdon, Bournemouth; and the Northcotes of Milnthorpe, Winchester. The Heathcotes and Northcotes were both Catholic families. James's sister Gertrude and Rix Northcote were close friends, travelling around by donkey cart.

The captions in italics on these two pages appear exactly as they were written in the album.

'Packham House' -
on the outskirts of Fordingbridge, now the Allenwater Nursing Home.

'Adm. Foley, F. Lambert, R. Foley, Fitz Lambert, Addy Foley, Fan F.' - the Admiral and his 'crew' on the River Avon!

'G.C., Adm. Foley, E. Stourton, Fan Foley, Alg. Foley' - sitting on the steps in front of Packham House.

'Sandhill Manor Farm' - actually Sandle Manor itself, a few years before its enlargement by the Hulse family.

'Miss Walker, Francis Lambert, G. Coventry, Everard Stourton, Fan Foley'

'Brookheath' - home of the Seton family and thus where James's mother was brought up.

ABOVE :
'Merdon, Bournemouth, Gilbert Heathcote'

ABOVE RIGHT :
'Sir William Heathcote and Pearl'

RIGHT :
'Isobel Heathcote'

The Heathcote family lived at Hursley Park, south of Winchester, from the 1720s. They held the Lordship of the Manor of Merdon, named from the nearby ruins of Merdon Castle. Their estate was sold in the 1880s, following the death of Sir William, the 5th baronet.

The Sir William photographed here is almost certainly the 6th baronet, having named his new Bournemouth home after the ancestral estates. *'Merdon'* and its grounds have, in recent times, been replaced by an estate of bungalows.

ABOVE LEFT :
'Milnthorpe, Winchester, Sybil Northcote'

ABOVE :
'G.C., B. Northcote, Pepper'

LEFT :
'Rix Northcote and Robin'

The Coventry Family's Home Town of Fordingbridge

Fordingbridge is a small town in the valley of the Hampshire Avon, on the western edge of the New Forest. In Victorian times, Burgate House and its park, lying just to the north-east of the historic core of the town, provided a focus for many important local events. (Today the house and the remnants of the park are cut off from the town by the 1970s by-pass.)

The parish church of St Mary's (above) is situated on the southern edge of the town; a church has existed on this site since Saxon times. However, much of the existing structure, including the north chapel, the east end of which can be seen beyond the chancel, dates from the thirteenth century. The splendid hammer-beam roof of the chapel dates from the late fifteenth century, as does the tower, which occupies an unusual position on the north side of the church. (1683)

The administration of Fordingbridge over many centuries was complicated by the division of the town into three manors. The Lords of the Manor of Fordingbridge were the Prideaux-Brunes, who lived in Cornwall, while the Rectory Manor came under the auspices of the Provost and Scholars of King's College, Cambridge. Thus the Coventrys, holding the Lordship of the third Manor, Burgate, were effectively the chief local gentry in the late nineteenth century.

The building facing the camera at the end of Salisbury Street, partially hidden by a canopy of lime trees, is the Old Court House of the Manor of Burgate, dating from about 1711, but incorporating earlier work.

The large building on the right of the picture was the Star Inn until October 1869. The cottages on the left were demolished many years ago, their site later being occupied by the town's Post Office. (1436)

Provost Street gained its name from the King's College connection.

With the exception of the nearest house on each side, all of the buildings seen in this photograph have since been replaced. The 17th-century tenements in the left foreground were typical of a large number of damp and dilapidated properties that were cleared away in the early years of the twentieth century. The Kings Arms Inn (on the right, with the large chimney) closed in 1869 and the site has been redeveloped in the 1990s. (HRO:25/68)

Just to the north of Fordingbridge parish church is Church Street, so broad that it is often referred to as 'Church Square'. This is probably where the town's first markets were held in the twelfth century. A footpath leading off the square is known as Chopys Lane - 'chopys' is a corruption of 'shops', the medieval name for market stalls.

By Victorian times, this had become the site of the September pleasure fair. In 1884, the local paper reported : *'There was a larger number of shows and stalls than have been seen here for some years. The principal sources of attraction as usual, were the steam roundabouts and swinging boats, which appeared to do a thriving trade.'*

The state of the streets before tarmac was introduced is clearly shown in this picture. Today, the scene is transformed with various forms of street furniture, but the external appearance of the houses on either side has changed little. (921)

Although most of Fordingbridge has always stood to the west of the River Avon, there has been a small group of houses known as Horseport on the other side of the Great Bridge, since at least the fourteenth century. The name seems evocative of former activity on the river, but the exact origin of the name is still uncertain.

The Victoria Rooms on the left were built in 1874 for plays, exhibitions, lectures and meetings - and are still used regularly today.

On the opposite side of the road, the house beyond the draper's shop is Bridge House. (1444)

The rear of Bridge House now has a rather different appearance from that seen in this photograph. This section of the River Avon was diverted when the Fordingbridge by-pass was constructed.

Bridge House is probably the best documented property in Fordingbridge with a continuous sequence of deeds and leases surviving from the fourteenth century. For a time in the seventeenth and eighteenth centuries it was an inn, known in turn as the *Little George* and the *Dolphin*. Many local people remember it as the doctors' surgery, before it was converted into flats in 1993. (1458)

This view of the Great Bridge at Fordingbridge, taken from what is now the Recreation Ground, has been painted and photographed many times. Burgate House, upstream from the bridge, had a boathouse (see page 22) and the family's rowing-boat appears in several of James's pictures. The cleric occupying the boat on this occasion was probably his brother Alexander Moray Coventry, who was a Catholic priest at Bognor Regis.

We do not know to what extent James's photography became more than a personal hobby. We know that he sometimes took portraits and scenes for friends – but this photograph and at least one other (Penton's Hill, Hyde, see page 41) were printed as picture post-cards and sold locally. They occasionally turn up in post-card sales. (1476)

As mentioned in the introduction, James inscribed a consecutive number on each of his quarter-plate glass negatives, up to a total of at least 5624. This photograph is taken from the earliest negative to survive, number 34. It may date from 1891, or possibly from as early as the summer of 1889.

The picture shows the family rowing boat again, on the Avon near Burgate House. Alexander is probably doing the rowing again, while the figure in the top hat seems to be a senior cleric, presumably a guest of the devout Catholic family. (34)

Fordingbridge Market Place, with the Crown Inn on the left, the Royal Arms on the right and the Town Hall with its clock tower in the centre.

From a prominent pole adjacent to the Royal Arms, a wire runs to the town's Post Office, the furthest building on the left, beyond the horse and cart. This was part of an early telephone line from the Post Office to the Railway Station, which had been installed in December 1870. A room just inside the Town Hall was established in December 1880 as 'Isaac Spratt's Coffee Room'. It opened at 5 a.m. to supply coffee, tea, cocoa and refreshments to men on their way to work. (1891)

The wisteria covered house is Fryern Court, just to the north of Fordingbridge and barely more than a mile from Burgate House. In medieval times the property was owned by the Cistercian monks of Beaulieu, and the name seems to mistakenly commemorate them as 'friars'.

In the 18th century it was the home of the Rookes and later the Reads. At the time of this photograph, the house was part of the Breamore Estate, the tenants being William and Mary Bond. The young boy at the window may be their eldest son, aged about four at the time of this photograph.

A more famous and more recent resident at Fryern Court was the painter Augustus John, who made his home and studio here from 1928 till 1961. He is now commemorated in Fordingbridge by a statue standing near the bridge.

Damerham, Rockbourne and Breamore

These three villages lie to the north and north-west of Fordingbridge and have always been very much part of the hinterland of the town. They must have been well-known to James; some of his most picturesque views were taken in this area.

This peaceful scene at Mill End, Damerham, with its thatched cottages and narrow, quiet street really does give an insight into a vanished age.

The building on the right of the picture was the old mill-house, now a private house. The wooden bridge seen in the foreground of the picture spanned the mill-leat – the channel which carried water to the mill-wheel. The cottage on the left has disappeared completely. Fire destroyed Miss Oxford's cottage (in the background) in 1976. It has since been rebuilt in a more modern style, with a tiled roof. (2257)

By the time that James reached South End at Damerham, five photographic exposures later, the sun was shining on what appears to have been a very pleasant late winter's day. The four women and girls in the foreground may well be James's relations, perhaps travelling with him in the donkey cart on this excursion. Two older men in the background are probably Damerham villagers. The vegetable garden in front of the further cottage has been dug over and prepared, ready for spring sowing and planting

The scene at South End looks rather different today. High bushes in the foreground obstruct the view from this camera position. The cottage in the background has gone - the photograph shows signs of deterioration in its walls. The nearer cottage has been extended and no longer has a thatched roof. (2264)

Rockbourne is considered to be one of the most attractive of Hampshire's villages, with its thatched cottages situated on either side of the village street and the chalk stream running alongside.

In the first of these delightful photographs it is clearly summertime. The trees are in full leaf, the roses are in flower and the roads are dry and free from winter mud. However, the stream, which sometimes dries up in summer, still has a flow of water. The group of local children are posing for James Coventry on the bridge which leads to the Baptist Chapel. Several adults are keeping an eye on them over the gate of Jade Cottage. (1809)

      The winter view of Rockbourne contrasts nicely with the one above. There is far more water in the chalk stream, as is usual in the wetter months. On the extreme left of the picture is a poster advertising the Fordingbridge Regatta – which must have remained on display from the previous summer. The small building with a tiled roof in the centre of the picture was the village blacksmith's. This disappeared long ago and the village's War Memorial now stands on the site. (2345)

      Although the two photographs of Rockbourne were taken several years apart, they were both taken from the same bridge, that which now forms the entrance to the house known as *Shearings*.

When James Coventry took this photograph of St Mary's Church at Breamore, no-one was aware of its Saxon origins. A previous restoration of 1874 had removed the coat of plaster from the chancel, revealing the flint walls beneath. It was not until a more major restoration of 1897, only a few years after James's visit, that late 10th-century arches and windows were revealed and the true antiquity of the building was discovered. At this time, the plaster was removed from the remainder of the outside walls.

One of the girls is sitting on a wooden grave marker, a type common in the 19th-century as a cheap alternative to stone. Sadly, none survive there today. (1580)

The church of St. Andrew's, Rockbourne, is set into the hillside above the village, with the adjoining Manor Farm just visible on the right. The church is early Norman in origin but has been altered and extended over the centuries, the small wooden tower dating from 1630. Restoration had been carried out and the south porch added in 1893 – the fabric of the church was clearly in good order at the time of this photograph. In the distance are the village's medieval open-fields bordering its extensive sheep downs, with Damerham Knoll on the horizon. (1626)

Breamore's village stocks stood on a green known as Little Marsh for centuries. Only one record of their use has survived: on 17th February 1586, John Cooke was *'whipped at the post'* then put into the stocks for four hours for the theft of a white horse. When the school grounds were enclosed in 1872, the stocks remained in the school garden. Today, following road widening, they stand on the roadside opposite the *Bat and Ball Hotel*.

The writing on an outhouse of the inn gives local results of the 1892 General Election. Edward Hulse had a majority of 238 as M.P. for Salisbury, while J. Scott-Montague had a majority of 755 in the New Forest Constituency and Lord Folkestone was elected M.P. for South Wiltshire, majority 268. (2177)

The rather unusual Georgian brick farmhouse at Court Farm, Damerham, contains a number of medieval windows. These must have been re-used from a known earlier building on the site. From at least the thirteenth century, the Court House and Grange of Glastonbury Abbey, which owned the village, were situated here. A splendid 14th-century Tithe Barn still survives nearby. (2329)

Farming Scenes

Photographs of agricultural scenes figure less prominently in James Coventry's work than one might expect. However, farming was very much part of his everyday life as estate manager - and how many of us photograph aspects of our everyday lives ?

The splendid scene in a Victorian farmstead (above) - and another shot of the same location which appears on page 6 - repays detailed study. The ladies and girls have been posed in the foreground, complete with baby wrapped in a shawl and tame sheep – but no-one could persuade all of the hens to remain still for the length of the exposure! In and around the farm buildings, note the chicken coop, wagons, staddle-stone barn, open-fronted shed and a pile of 'faggots' for winter fuel. Next to the farmhouse with its creeper over the door is a long thatched barn with open stable doors. All in all, an idyllic picture, perhaps deliberately so, of the type of mixed farming which was once very much the norm.

　　　The hill in the background is reminiscent of Whitsbury or Stuckton, but the actual location of these buildings is uncertain. Probably most have now gone and the house, if it still stands, may no longer be part of a farmstead. (2234)

Scenes similar to the one below were commonplace on all the chalk downlands from the Middle Ages into the twentieth century. This large flock of Hampshire Down sheep, accompanied by its solitary shepherd, is on Rockbourne Down. The mound on the left is the Neolithic long-barrow known as Duck's Nest; the tree-capped hillock in the distance, to the south-west, is Damerham Knoll. Today, most of this land is arable, Duck's Nest is covered in trees and scrub; and this view is blocked by a large hedge at the point where James was standing. (2311)

Thatched Cottages and the Lives of the Rural Cottagers

At the small hamlet of Outwick in Breamore parish, the gentry meet the cottagers! Three young girls are sitting in the tub-cart drawn by a donkey, attended by one of James' female relations. On the other side of the road, another girl holds a baby, a young lad looks on, while, on the far right of the picture, one of the cottagers peers at the photographer round a bush.

Outwick has a long and interesting history. There were Iron Age and Roman settlements and a medieval hamlet nearby. In the middle of the nineteenth century, over eighty people lived here, but today only four houses remain. Of the buildings in the picture, only the cottage on the right survives. (1693)

The photograph below is extremely evocative of the way of life of the ordinary villagers in the 1890s. The back gardens of these three terraced cottages are typical of the vegetable plots which were vital to the livelihoods of the poorer villagers for centuries. Washlines are prominent features, while tubs and buckets lie around. Three adults and six children all stare at the strange sight of the photographer busy with his equipment!

The location is not certain, but this is thought also to have been at Outwick, where a group of cottages was burnt down early in the twentieth century. (2036)

Another rather dilapidated-looking thatched cottage, another vegetable garden, another group of villagers watching the photographer. The man of the house seems rather resentful of this intrusion into his domain by a member of the gentry!

Swedes are growing in the foreground, and there appear to be raspberry canes in front of the chicken-run and the open sided cart shelter. What seems to be the front door of the cottage is unusually at the end of the building. There is a field or meadow at the back, with open heathland beyond. (2266)

Most of the pictures in this book are reproduced from modern prints, taken from the negatives which were processed by James Coventry himself. Very few prints made by him survive. If those in the extant album were printed by James, they are among his earlier work. The photograph below, however, is reproduced from a print undoubtedly produced by James in his darkroom. It is a contact print (made to the same size, directly from the negative), mounted on a board measuring 6 by 5¼ inches. It is now in the possession of Mrs A Crouter of Gorley near Fordingbridge. Family tradition states that it is by James Coventry and the style is undoubtedly his.

The picture shows the garden of William Roberts at a cottage in North Gorley called *The Apiary* - note the beehives on the left. The girl in the foreground is Mrs Crouter's mother, Henrietta Roberts, then aged about 8. The second girl is Henrietta's sister, Edith, aged about 11.

The cottage in these two pictures is believed to have been at Harbridge. The same three girls appear in both pictures, although the photographs were taken several weeks apart.

In the upper picture, the girls are playing with large dolls, apparently on a newly dug-over plot! In the second picture, they are in the field adjoining the garden, and one of them appears to be picking blackberries. (1697 above ; 1750 below)

Unfortunately, we have not been able to identify these two cottages, but the photographs have been included for their pictorial quality.

Of the six children in the upper picture, three have lost interest in the camera and tripod, in fact two have moved during the exposure. An older girl looks on behind the hedge. The cottage appears more prosperous than some, with a neat fence and topiary in the garden. (2321)

In the lower picture, the cottage takes second place to the splendid image of a young 'nanny' with two children in her care, using a pram which would be a real antique today. (2576)

Scenes from the New Forest

While Fordingbridge has never been within the perambulation (the traditional boundary) of the New Forest, the town and its inhabitants have always had very close links with the Forest.

The most convenient aproach to the open heathlands of the Forest, then as now, would be to take the road rising up out of the Avon Valley to the village of Godshill. This route passes the large house called *Avonside*, part of the hamlet of Criddlestyle.

Avonside, shown here from the south-east, was built a little before 1875 for Henry Thompson, a farmer and member of a prominent local family. When this picture was taken, more than twenty years later, it was probably occupied by a Mr Lawrence Peel. Perhaps the couple in the picture are Mr and Mrs Peel. (1512)

No doubt the Coventry family, with more leisure time than their less affluent contemporaries, made many excursions into the Forest, by carriage, on foot, by bicycle - or, as here, on horseback. This is the lane, now a busy B road, leading to Godshill.

The entrance to *Avonside* is just visible on the right. The flat hilltop beyond the trees was the site of an Iron Age and Roman settlement, whilst the terraces visible on the slope are gardens belonging to a nearby 18th-century cottage. (1598)

To the south-east of Fordingbridge, on the edge of the New Forest, is a group of villages and hamlets – Stuckton, Frogham, Blissford, Hyde, Ogdens, Hungerford. Many of the holdings have commoners' rights in the Forest.

Blissford Hill, on the road down from Frogham, has a gradient of one-in-three, but appears misleadingly gentle here. In the days before it was given a tarmac coating, it posed considerable difficulties for most vehicles. The cottages have all been demolished or replaced since James Coventry's visit but in many other respects little has changed. (1745)

LEFT : This lane, running along the northern edge of Hyde Common, has seen few alterations over the past century, although the houses have, of course, been modernised.

The nearest one on the right is known as Winnie Bush's Cottage. Surprisingly the horse-chestnut tree standing in the lane in the middle distance is still there. (1817)

The photograph below is the second of James's pictures known to have been published as picture postcards in about 1905 (see pages 12 and 29).

The two girls in the photograph appear to be fascinated by something; close study of the original suggests that this is a group of about six or eight tiny ducklings.

Behind the girls are two of the old foresters' cottages at the top of Penton's Hill on the edge of Hyde Common. The cottage in the foreground is known as *Hannington's*. Clearly the older part, nearer the lane, was constructed of cob and thatch on a brick foundation. (Cob is a traditional New Forest building material composed of clay and straw.) At the back, it has a 19th-century brick and slate extension. The further cottage no longer exists. (2437)

This superb Forest-edge view was taken from Hyde Common looking south-eastwards. Beyond the small thatched cottage, there is a patchwork of fields, some arable, some pasture, most of which survives today.

Each smallholder would use a few of these fields and would also pasture animals on the heathland of the open Forest, which can be seen in the distance. The woodland on the slightly higher ground is Hasley Inclosure. (2071)

In this view, we are looking north-eastwards from near Folds Farm towards Godshill Wood. It is probable that the brook in the foreground is the one called Salverhooke in the earliest surviving perambulation of the New Forest, dating from 1217-18. At this time and for many years after, the stream formed part of the boundary of the Forest. (1746)

Another New Forest view, this time south-westwards from the road between Hyde and Ogdens, on the edge of the New Forest. The area below the cottages is known as Holland Bottom, with South Gorley in the distance. (1668)

New Forest ponies and cattle have special spots, known as shades, where they gather on hot days. A brook or pool in which to stand provides an additional opportunity to cool off. Ponies and cattle still gather in the little valley of Latchmoor Bottom near Ogdens. The nearby car park is now a popular base for exploring the Forest on foot. Sloden Inclosure is in the distance, and Hasley Hill on the right. (1115)

The stream in the upper photograph is the Latchmoor Brook, which rises near Bramshaw Telegraph and runs through three large Inclosures before flowing through the heathland of Latchmoor Bottom. Below Ogdens, its name changes to the Huckles Brook. The small footbridge (below) crosses it near Furzehill, with Dorridge Hill Clump in the background. The stream eventually discharges into the Avon not far from the farm and garage which are named after it.

There is a bicycle leaning against the end of the bridge – did James sometimes carry his photographic equipment in this way? His quarter-plate camera, when folded, was small for its day, but a wooden tripod would not have been easy to transport on a bicycle, especially over open heathland! On the other hand, is this the same young lady using the same man's bicycle as in the photograph on page 19 ? (2564)

Five of James Coventry's young ladies pose in this photograph, two of them standing on top of 'The Butt', a Bronze Age round barrow near Fritham. It survives today, despite the fact that much of the area became an airfield during the Second World War.

   The open heathland here was already popular for day trips and picnics in James's day and is still much frequented by summer visitors and locals alike. The Stoney Cross road can be seen in the background, behind the trees on the left. (3942)

Nomansland seems a typical New Forest village. Almost all of its houses, however, are just outside the Forest perambulation – and indeed are across the county boundary in Wiltshire – while the adjoining woodland and grazing land, including the village cricket field, are in the Forest. The villagers were outside the jurisdiction of the forest keepers; they owed allegiance to no man, hence the name.

   This view is still very recognisable today with the large oak tree dominating the junction of two minor roads. The thatched house on the left has gone and the Nomansland Garage now adjoins its former front garden. The first hand-operated petrol pumps appeared here in 1912, while the garage site was used to store the rides of Coles Funfair during the Second World War. (3964)

This view of beech pollards, taken in Ridley Wood, north of Burley in the New Forest, is representative of a large number of 'tree portraits' taken by James Coventry. (Over twenty negatives survive which were taken here or in nearby Verely Wood.)

Ridley is a good example of the Ancient and Ornamental Woodlands of the New Forest, which are unfenced and thus regularly grazed by the commoners' ponies and cattle. Grazed woodland is, in modern times, a very unusual habitat with few other examples in Europe. Ridley is dominated by beech trees, with some oaks and a shrub layer of holly.

Most of the beeches at Ridley, like that on the right, have many branches, dividing from the trunk ten or more feet above the ground, a clear indication that they have been pollarded. As pollarding, to provide leaves for animal fodder, was banned in the Forest in 1698, trees with this appearance today must be well over 300 years old. (1291)

While the photograph above was clearly taken in winter, this is a summertime view, with sunlight dappling the ground through the leaves of the oak trees and the bracken in full growth.

In one of the Coventry albums seen by Philip Allison in the 1970s, this shot was captioned 'Godshill Wood'. In contrast to the 'A and O Woodlands', this is an Inclosure - a wood which is fenced to prevent grazing by domestic animals. (1130)

The Avon Valley

Fordingbridge lies in the valley of the Hampshire Avon which flows south into Christchurch harbour. In this section is a collection of photographs taken between Burgate, only a few miles south of the Wiltshire border, and Christchurch.

Other photographs taken in the valley, northwards towards Salisbury, appear in the Wiltshire section.

At least two of these views (opposite and above) of flooded watermeadows were taken from the front lawns of Burgate House, looking across the Avon Valley towards Godshill. It seems probable that this was the great flood of November 1894 which resulted from over eleven inches of rain falling in five weeks. (954, 955, 956)

Another example of the power of the weather to change the appearance of the landscape. This tree was snapped off by a winter gale – perhaps the great gale of 2nd-3rd March 1897. It probably stood somewhere on the Burgate Estate, which James was largely responsible for managing from about 1877 till his father's death in 1897. (1575)

OPPOSITE, ABOVE : Just south of Fordingbridge is the village of Bickton, with a mill whose origins can be traced back to late Saxon times when the owner of the village was named Chetel.

The existing building dates from the nineteenth century. This photograph, featuring the inevitable little girls, is taken from upstream. At the time of James Coventry's visit, the long-established owners of the mill were J R Neave & Co, producers of a widely acclaimed 'farinaceous baby food'. Like most mills in recent times, it has found other uses, in this case conversion to maisonettes and a trout farm. (1739)

OPPOSITE, BELOW : A little downstream of the mill is Bickton Farm, home of successive Lords of the Manor for several centuries. In the sixteenth century, there was '*a greate bell hanging in the roffe of the said manor house wyche of a veri long tyme had hanged there and used as a warnyng bell when any daunger of enemyes fyer or theves were abought the said house'.* Its effectiveness against 'theves' was not great – the bell itself was stolen in 1560 ! (1634)

ABOVE : An eel-trap on the River Avon, perhaps at East Mill near Fordingbridge, where one was marked on an early Ordnance Survey map. The river has long been a prolific source of eels; in fact, in Saxon times many of the mills on the river paid at least part of their rent in eels. (694)

This view of the village street at Bickton is one of the photographs from a lost Coventry album, copied by Philip Allison in the 1970s.

He included eight of James's photographs in *The New Forest – A Photographic Record of 100 Years of Forest Life*. (See Appendix.) (PA6/50)

Ibsley village is situated about half-way between Fordingbridge and Ringwood. The core of the old village, with several picturesque thatched cottages, including the *Old Beams Inn*, stands alongside the main road. Some of them can be seen in the background of this photograph, taken from the watermeadows. (2494)

Ibsley Bridge, just upstream of the weir in the upper photograph, gives access via a causeway to the village of Harbridge. This route forms the only public vehicular crossing of the Avon between Fordingbridge and Ringwood – it must have been an important route for centuries. The meadows on either side of the causeway, a well-known winter grazing area for large numbers of Bewick's Swans, are frequently flooded.

The old bridge photographed by James Coventry was replaced by the existing stone bridge in 1930. (2493)

TOP : James's young friend is standing in the watermeadows by the Ibsley-Harbridge causeway mentioned opposite.

In the background, where the ground rises up from the flood-plain, Harbridge Rectory (still used for that purpose at the time of James's visit) partially blocks the view of All Saints' Church. The tiny village of Harbridge is known to date from Saxon times; but the present church was built in 1838. The architect, G Evans, retained only the stonework of the lower section of the tower from a previous building of 1450. (1971)

RIGHT : At Harbridge School, the boys and girls were carefully segregated for James's photograph. The building, a private dwelling today, is within the Somerley estate. (1696)

RIGHT, BELOW : The hamlet of South Gorley is on the minor road connecting Fordingbridge and Ringwood – a road which forms the western boundary of the New Forest. Its village green, with a small pond, is an attractive spot, often frequented by Forest ponies.

A village school was built on the edge of the green in 1874, at the expense of the Earl of Normanton. Provision was made for eighty pupils although the average attendance at this time was 72. Around the time of James Coventry's visit, the school-mistress was Mrs Harriet Head. The school was closed many years ago and is now a private house. (1650)

Young girls, water and trees – three of the favourite elements in a James Coventry photograph! And if one or more of his models could be persuaded to poke about in the water with a long stick, so much the better !

The upper photograph is at the footbridge over the Hamer Brook near Plumley Farm, on the Somerley Estate north of Ringwood. The lower one may be nearer the family home at Burgate. (1492 and 1752)

Moyles Court is a pleasant spot on the edge of the New Forest – but it was the scene of a tragic event in 1685.

At this time, the house, a fine mid-17th-century brick edifice, was the home of Dame Alice Lisle, a 70-year-old widow. After the Battle of Sedgemoor, she innocently gave shelter to a fugitive from the Monmouth Rebellion. She was arrested for harbouring a traitor and was tried under Judge Jefferies at the infamous 'Bloody Assize'. He sentenced her to be burnt alive that very day. Thanks to the intervention of the Bishop of Winchester, the sentence was 'commuted' to one of beheading, which was carried out on 2nd September in Winchester market-place. Her grave lies in the parish churchyard at Ellingham. A nearby public house is named the *Alice Lisle*.

Moyles Court house (top) is now a co-educational private school, taking day pupils and boarders between the ages of four and 16. (1724)

Near Moyles Court house, and by a junction of minor roads leading to Ellingham, South Gorley, Linwood and Ringwood, there is a well-known water-splash (centre). Beside it stands the 'Moyles Court Oak', even larger today than when it was photographed by James Coventry (bottom).

Both scenes are still easily recognisable. Although the ford has been provided with a concrete base more suited to modern traffic, cars frequently have to drive through several inches of water. The spot is a popular family stopping place in summer, with children paddling in the stream. It can become quite crowded – especially when the ice-cream van is in attendance! (1726 & 1727.)

53

Ringwood, like Fordingbridge to the north, was always an important crossing point of the Avon, with the whole of the town lying to the east of the river. This view is looking up West Street, across one of the branches of the river towards the Market Place, always considered the most photogenic view of the town. Hens are pecking around at the water's edge.

The street was called Wimborne Road, and it was the main road out of town to the west before the modern A31 by-pass was built. The tower of the church, Saint Peter and Saint Paul, which was completely rebuilt in the 1850s, can be seen to the left of the thatched roof. On the original print, the Jubilee lamp, erected in the Market Place in 1887, is just visible. (1986)

The old Wimborne Road out of Ringwood, beyond the main branch of the River Avon, crossed the King Stream on this brick bridge. The scene is very different today, as the A31 at this point is a major dual carriageway, with two lanes westbound and four lanes eastbound! This view is from the south with the tree line on the left horizon being the Ringwood Forest.

On the original negative, a skein of geese, flying in V-formation, can just be distinguished above the figures on the bridge. (2319)

The village of Sopley lies in the Avon Valley about two miles north of Christchurch. The mill, seen on the left of this picture, bears a date of 1878, the year in which it was enlarged by F W Bemister. He was still the owner when this photograph was taken. It finally closed in 1946 but now houses a restaurant. Due to the growth of vegetation on the river bank, it is now impossible to photograph both mill and church in the same shot. (1970)

The church of St. Michael stands on a large mound, which may be artificial, overlooking the River Avon. Much of the church dates from the thirteenth and fourteenth centuries, but it was re-roofed in 1893, following storm damage. Interesting internal furnishings include two life-size Purbeck marble effigies dating from the thirteenth century and a fine Jacobean wooden pulpit of 1604. (1969)

Around Christchurch

Christchurch Priory is a former monastic church which, following the Dissolution, survived as the town's parish church. King Henry VIII issued Letters Patent on 23rd October 1540 granting the church to the churchwardens and parishioners - the precise wording of the gift was : *'choir, body, bell tower with seven bells, stones, timber, lead of roofing and gutter of the Church and cemetery on the north side'.* The earliest church on this site dated from 650 A D, while the present building was commenced in 1094. The tall tower which is a landmark for miles around was added in the fifteenth century.

Christchurch was formerly known as Twynham, 'the place between two rivers', where the Stour and the Avon flow together to form Christchurch Harbour. When James Coventry took this photograph, he was standing on the southern shore of the tidal Stour estuary, on land which is now private; but a similar view can be seen today from the footpath between Wick Lane and Hengistbury Head. (875)

Throop Mill on the River Stour is now on the northern outskirts of Bournemouth. This picture was taken at an intermediate stage of its rebuilding during the summer of 1902 - the left-hand section has been modernised, the right-hand half awaits reconstruction. The millers at the time were Thomas Whicher & Co. Their wagon, standing under the open doorway, is loaded with sacks of flour ready for delivery. The other cart belongs to a local firm of building contractors. Much of the mill machinery, made by Armfields of Ringwood, has been restored in recent years and the mill is now open to the public from time to time during the summer. (4540)

Hengistbury Head is a promontory separating Christchurch Harbour from the English Channel. Being composed largely of sands which overlay a band of clay, its southern shore is being eroded constantly by the sea. Over the past two centuries the shoreline has moved back more than 160 yards. Probably almost a third of this has gone since this photo was taken.

The whole headland is protected both as a nature reserve and as an ancient monument. Throughout the Iron Age, Hengistbury was an important port, as has been shown by extensive excavations over the past century. From about 150 BC, trading connections were established with many parts of Europe, imports including fine pottery, glass vessels and jewellery. The Iron Age inhabitants of the headland were protected by a great double earth rampart, much of which can still be seen today. (1590)

This large house on the cliffs at Southbourne, near Christchurch, was built in about 1890 and became known as Southbourne House. It was one of the first houses on the still largely undeveloped heathlands here, and must have had superb views eastwards to Hengistbury and the Isle of Wight and south-westwards to Purbeck. The house no longer exists, having been demolished prior to the construction of Southbourne Coast Road with its numerous cliff-top villas. (1585)

Two posed shots at the seaside. Could the group of eleven young girls on a rather stony beach, photographed in about 1900, be the Catholic schoolgirls from Fordingbridge on their annual outing ? Note the steamer on the horizon in the upper photograph. (PA 3/51 and PA 3/61)

The Isle of Wight

These two views of Freshwater Bay, Isle of Wight, are among the latest photographs of Coventry's which are preserved, probably dating from the summer of 1903. We wonder if James Coventry's visit to Freshwater Bay was something of a pilgrimage to the former home of the famous Victorian portrait photographer, Julia Margaret Cameron. Her house, Dimbola Lodge, not far from the bay, is now a photographic museum and gallery.

These two pictures are of historic interest, revealing the speed of erosion of the island's shores. Of the two stacks to be seen in the upper photograph, the right hand one is Stag Rock. According to tradition it acquired this name after a stag hunt in the seventeenth century – the quarry had escaped, temporarily, by leaping onto the rock. The headland faintly visible to the right of Stag Rock is Hanover Point. (4984)

The left-hand stack is Arch Rock (also seen in the lower photograph). It collapsed on 25th October 1992 at 8.50 am, as storms lashed the south coast of the island. Only a small rocky slab remains, covered at the highest tides. However, today another stack is to be seen; Mermaid Rock was formed in 1967 by the collapse of part of the main cliff. (4977)

Romsey Abbey

James Coventry visited Romsey on at least two occasions, possibly more; two of the four existing negatives depicting the Abbey are among the eight in the HRO collection which do not bear numbers.

The original abbey was founded by King Edward the Elder in the early years of the tenth century. The Norman abbey church, dedicated to Saints Mary and Ethelflaeda, was built between 1120 and 1250, the third church on the site. It was perhaps commenced partly as Henry I's memorial to Queen Matilda, who had been educated at the Abbey.

The community of Benedictine nuns continued to be a dominant part of life in the town until the Dissolution in 1539. While the other abbey buildings – dormitory, refectory, cloisters, abbess's house and so on – disappeared over the years, the abbey church was purchased by the town from Henry VIII in 1544 for the sum of £100. Like the Priory at Christchurch, it has been the town's parish church ever since. It is widely considered to be one of the finest pieces of Norman ecclesiastical architecture to be seen in England.

OPPOSITE, ABOVE : The view of the Abbey from the north shows the graveyard before all the tombstones were removed and used to make a pathway. Romsey's parish church of St Lawrence, from about 1400 till 1544, consisted of the north aisle and north transept of the abbey church, plus an additional parallel aisle. The opening up of the existing aisle and transept into this extension, and its subsequent demolition following the Dissolution, has resulted in the rather muddled architectural appearance of the north aisle. The North Porch was built in 1907 and thus does not appear here. (HRO:25/69)

OPPOSITE, BELOW : This view of the east end of the Abbey was taken from Church Place. The church once extended further eastwards with twin Lady Chapels, which were demolished before the Dissolution. The two large windows in the Decorated style are placed within blank round-headed Norman arches. (1468)

ABOVE : Romsey Abbey seen from the south-east, with a terrace called Temple Buildings, dating from 1820, on the right of the picture. The modern visitor walking along the street known as The Meads cannot see this view due to subsequent development. (533)

BELOW : In the angle of the south transept and the south aisle is the Abbess's doorway. At this time the fine Norman decoration of the arch was badly damaged; the line of a former lean-to roof can be seen. Until Rev Berthon, the enterprising vicar of Romsey from 1860-92, began to restore the Abbey to its former glory, a rag-and-bone merchant plied his trade in this lean-to! On the transept wall is a very fine Saxon rood, which originally adorned the earlier church on the site and which dates from about 1000 AD. (HRO:25/70)

Visits to other Landed Gentry

The Coventry family were important members of the landed gentry in their home area. No doubt their social scene involved many visits to others who were in similar strata of society.

These visits would have been made either on horseback or in some form of carriage. On page 18, we have seen two of the ladies of the household with a donkey-drawn gig. For larger parties in the summer or for visits further afield (for example to Stonehenge, see page 70) a Victoria carriage or phaeton would have been more suitable.

The picture above was captioned *'Penney and Cob'* in the 1880s album, but there appear to be no records of a coachman on the Coventry staff or of a Mr Penney living in the area. (The Coventry household in 1891 included a butler, a cook, a housemaid and a kitchen maid. A gardener occupied the Gardener's Cottage and two general labourers lived in the two lodges.)

The photograph below shows the entrance to West Park at Rockbourne, the home of the Eyre Coote family. These lodges remain today, in a dilapidated state, but West Park House was demolished in 1948. (2465)

Somerley House, north of Ringwood, was purchased in 1828, along with a large estate, by the 2nd Earl of Normanton. It remains with the same family today.

The earliest reference to the Manor of Somerley dates from 1272, when the owner was Thomas Baldwin. The present house, with its terraces looking towards the River Avon, was designed between 1792 and 1795 by Samuel Wyatt for Mr David Hobson, though there have been subsequent alterations and additions. The house is not open to the public, but special events are sometimes held in the grounds. (1135)

This lodge, alongside the Ringwood to Verwood road, stands at the south-western entrance to the Somerley Estate. Formerly called the Ringwood Lodge, it is now known as Ashley Lodge. (918)

The Coventrys seem always to have been close friends of the Hulses of Breamore House, their nearest neighbours (amongst the gentry) to the north. The Elizabethan mansion was built by William Dodington in the 1580s. Following a series of tragedies afflicting the Dodington family, the house was bought by Sir Edward Hulse in 1748 and has been the family home ever since. The House is open to the public in the summer months.

These four young girls are at the back of Breamore House, just to the right of the present-day entrance porch. The window of the Inner Hall is behind them. The balustrade on which two of them are sitting guarded an open drop to the cellar passage below. This has subsequently been roofed in and the balustrade removed. (1648)

The lime avenue on the terrace to the north of Breamore House with Edward Hulse, later the 6th Baronet, and his black terrier dog. The avenue was planted in about 1810 and some of the trees have recently reached the end of their life. (2314)

Teffont Evias lies in the wooded Wiltshire valley of the River Nadder some nine miles west of Salisbury. The Tudor manor-house pictured here has had Gothic style towers added, and the view has changed little during the past century. The adjoining parish church with its tall spire was rebuilt in Victorian times. (1276)

Lady Adela Goff of Hale House was a friend of the Coventry family and is pictured here in a gig in Moot Lane, which runs along the eastern side of the Avon Valley between Woodgreen and Downton.

The path behind the pony leads steeply up to Hale church; it now forms a small part of the Avon Valley Path, a 26-mile waymarked route from Salisbury to Christchurch.

St Mary's Church, Hale, stands on the site of a medieval chapel which was owned by Breamore Priory until 1536. The present-day church exhibits a variety of architectural styles. Thomas Archer, a well-known 18th-century architect, lived in nearby Hale House; in about 1715, he radically changed the appearance of the church, while retaining earlier stonework in the nave and chancel. In Victorian times a number of Gothic features were added. Even in winter, the church is now almost hidden by vegetation from this spot. (1261)

Trafalgar House near Downton is a red-brick mansion which was designed in 1733 by Roger Morris for the banker Sir Peter Vanderput. Known originally as Standlynch House, its name was changed after it was presented to the Rev William Nelson, brother of Admiral Lord Nelson. He was also paid an annual pension in grateful recognition of his brother's achievements for the nation. Members of the Nelson family still lived in the house at the time of James Coventry's visit; it took an Act of Parliament in 1947 to end the pension and to enable the house to be sold. (By this time, the cost of maintaining the house had become an embarassment to the Nelson famly.) (2548)

Longleat House near Warminster was built between 1567 and 1580 by Sir John Thynne. The present owner, the unconventional 7th Marquess of Bath, is the fourteenth generation of his family to live there since its completion.

In the late eighteenth century, the grounds were said to include an aviary almost as large as Salisbury Market Place, containing upwards of eight thousand birds of many types. Today, the extensive grounds are famous as a 'safari park' and, along with the house, are visited by many thousands of people each year. (4949)

Wiltshire

The part of Hampshire around Fordingbridge is very close to the borders of both Wiltshire and Dorset, so it is hardly surprising that photographs taken in these two counties figure quite prominently in the collection of James Coventry's negatives. Downton and Salisbury were particularly easy of access, having a direct rail link from Fordingbridge.

ABOVE : Seven miles south of Salisbury, a public footpath leads eastwards from the village of Charlton-All-Saints, across the flood plain of the River Avon, towards the woodland surrounding Trafalgar House. The main channel of the river is crossed by this long foot-bridge, above a double weir – the scene has changed little since James photographed it about one hundred years ago. (1068)

The second picture was taken on the same visit, about three-quarters of a mile to the north. In one of the Coventry albums, it was captioned *'Blue Bridge, Trafalgar'*.

This fine brick-built bridge crosses one of the minor channels of the river at the eastern edge of the valley. Just out of sight up the slope stood Standlynch Dairy, part of the Trafalgar Estate; no doubt the bridge was regularly used by herds of cows returning to the water-meadows after morning and evening milking. Today, the spot is little visited and the bridge has almost disappeared under vegetation. (1071)

At the time of James's visit, the landscape garden known as 'The Moot' at Downton belonged to Mr E P Squarey of Moot House. He frequently allowed the amphitheatre shown in this picture to be used for public events such as fetes and open-air Shakespearean productions. In 1908, no less an actress than Miss Sybil Thorndike played Adriana in 'The Comedy of Errors' here.

The Moot, however, has a much older history. Local tradition has it that the garden is named from the location of the Saxon *moot* or meeting place for the Hundred of Downton. Henri de Blois, Bishop of Winchester, built a castle on the site in the early twelfth century.

The surviving motte and bailey earthworks of the castle were landscaped as a private pleasure garden in about 1725, when these ascending turf terraces were created. At the highest point there was a hexagonal Greek-style temple, of which only traces of the foundations may be seen today.

In the 1970s and 1980s, the garden was allowed to return to nature. Following further damage in the 'great gale' of October 1987, a Trust was formed to restore the garden, which is now permanently open to the public. (1065)

This view from The Moot shows Downton's parish church of St Lawrence. Although it mostly dates from the twelfth century, with a 14th-century chancel, it was restored in 1860.

Downton was once a market town, returning two members to Parliament before the Reform Act of 1832. The church stands in the heart of the original settlement of Saxon and Norman times, but in the thirteenth century the Bishop of Winchester, as Lord of the Manor, built a new planned borough to the west of the river to enlarge the town. This area, with its broad greensward and thatched cottages, is still known as The Borough. (1067)

There has been a tannery industry alongside the millstream at Downton since at least the eighteenth century; the owner recorded in 1793 was a Mr John Gibbs.

The old Tannery House and the jumble of buildings on the left were pulled down soon after the First World War to make way for those which dominate this scene today. (1063)

RIGHT : A track on the chalk downs looking towards the small Iron Age hill-fort known as Clearbury Rings. It lies in Odstock parish above the valley of the River Ebble, about three miles south of Salisbury.

The earthwork consists of a single bank and ditch with a causewayed entrance at the northern end of the south-west side. It is a prominent landmark throughout much of the area. (1079)

BELOW : Nunton is a small village, three miles south of Salisbury, situated in the valley of the River Ebble, not far from the point at which it joins the Avon. The church is beautifully situated in the valley and is now much more open to view, as the trees in the foreground of the picture are no longer present.

The existing church building was only about forty years old at the time of James Coventry's visit, having been almost completely rebuilt in 1854-5.

Dedicated to St Andrew, the building has never been a parish church. It was a Chapel of Ease of Downton parish and at the time of James's visit the incumbent was Rev Arthur Du Boulay Hill who lived in Downton. In 1915 Nunton and the adjoining village of Odstock were linked as a single parish. (4953)

It was Dr. Johnson who wrote, after visiting Salisbury Cathedral in the morning and Stonehenge in the afternoon, that 'Salisbury Cathedral and its neighbour Stonehenge, are two eminent models of art and rudeness, and may show the first essay, and the last perfection in architecture'.

Stonehenge in Victorian times was part of the private estate of the Antrobus family, but it was situated on uncultivated downland, open to all comers. While the numbers of visitors must have been far fewer than the thousands of tourists who visit today, the 'Stonehenge excursion' was a popular one, with carriages available for hire from Salisbury Station. An unofficial guardian may have been on hand to regale visitors with tales of Druids, but there were no refreshment facilities and a picnic hamper was a normal accompaniment on such a trip.

     The Coventrys had evidently arrived by horse-drawn phaeton – but there are other less obvious features in this picture. An additional horse is grazing on the far left; there is a photographer's tripod near the two gentlemen standing near the carriage; and there is a bicycle leaning behind one pair of stones. (1814)

This classic and much photographed view of Salisbury Cathedral is taken from Long Bridge at the Salisbury end of the Harnham watermeadows. Today the left bank of the River Nadder is a little less overgrown here as the area has been made into the Elizabeth Gardens, much used by both locals and tourists, especially on hot summer days. (876)

Salisbury Cathedral is unique among medieval English cathedrals in that it was built almost as a single conception, rather than added to in differing styles over many centuries. With the foundation stone laid on Easter Monday 1220, the building was ready for consecration by Boniface, Archbishop of Canterbury, only 38 years later.

Such unity, in the style now called Early English, accounts for the unsurpassed elegance of the edifice. The spire was added a little later, probably between 1300 and 1330.

Work continued on the imposing west front for several years after the Cathedral's consecration. The eighty figures seen in niches on the frontage were mostly 1860s replacements for the original medieval statues - at the time of writing, a thorough restoration is once again underway. (2424)

In this view, we see the Cathedral with the lower part of the spire encased in wooden scaffolding, photographed from the gardens at the rear of the North Canonry. Major repairs were undertaken in 1896 and this photo must date from the summer of that year. (1356)

A beautiful summer's day in the West Walk of The Close at Salisbury. The imposing gates in the foreground belong to *Arundells*, now the home of the former Prime Minister, Sir Edward Heath. Behind the carriage is the frontage of the North Canonry, built originally for resident canons of the Cathedral.

The Coventrys sometimes visited The Close, driving to Salisbury in a pony cart. They had friends there, members of the Purvis family, who were related to the Foleys of Packham House, Fordingbridge. (1348)

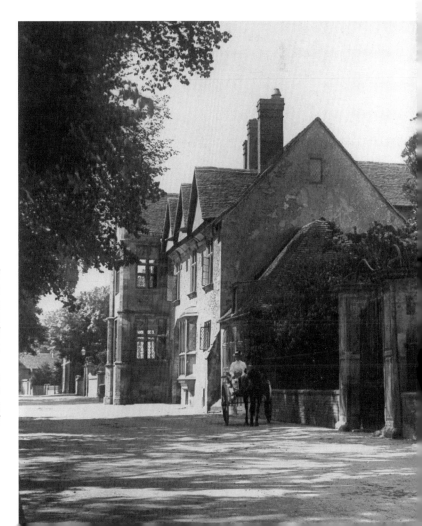

Four major tributaries join the River Avon at or near Salisbury. The stream which flows down from a north-easterly direction, through the Winterbourne villages, is the River Bourne. Milford Bridge, seen in this picture, lies about three-quarters of a mile east of Salisbury city centre. This medieval bridge formerly carried all the city's traffic to or from the east. The view is looking upstream with Laverstock Down beyond. (1350)

This second picture of the River Bourne at Milford was taken three exposures later than the one above, this time looking downstream. The scene is still recognisable today despite the inevitable changes to the flora. The tall building, just visible through the trees in the centre of the picture, was the then newly constructed Waterloo Flour Mill, alongside Milford Goods Yard. It survives today as the Tintometer Factory. (1353)

The success of medieval Salisbury as a 'new town' was dependant on a number of factors. Not least was the construction of Harnham Bridge over the Avon in 1244, a project instigated by Bishop Robert Bingham.

Prior to this date, most north-south traffic in the area used the bridge at Wilton. Following the construction of Harnham Bridge, many travellers used the new route, with the result that the importance of Wilton declined and trade in Salisbury increased. For many centuries this remained the only route into Salisbury from the south. (1355)

The River Ebble is generally thought of as one of Salisbury's 'five rivers', even though it does not flow through the city, joining the Avon about three miles to the south. This bridge over the Ebble at Coombe Bissett, dating from about 1780, carried the Salisbury to Blandford Turnpike for much of the nineteenth century.

The village took its name from the Old English *cumb* meaning valley, and from a local land-owning family of the twelfth and thirteenth centuries, the Bissetts. Bridge House beyond still survives, next to the well-known *Fox and Goose* public house. (5051)

Dorset

Based on the evidence of the existing collection of negatives, Portland and Weymouth may have been James Coventry's 'furthest west'.

The scene in this photograph taken at Weymouth is very different today. The wooden railway bridge seen in the picture crossed the River Wey at the point where Radipole Lake Swannery meets the Inner Harbour. It carried the line from Weymouth Town Station to Portland. The train on the right was on another line, from Weymouth Town to Weymouth Harbour. This ran along Commercial Road, which at that time formed the 'shoreline' of the Inner Harbour.

The bridge was replaced by an iron one in 1909; the passenger service to Portland ended in 1952; and the line was finally closed in 1965. The railway bridge was subsequently replaced by the road bridge, known as Swannery Bridge, which carries much of the traffic into Weymouth town centre today.

In the 1920s land was reclaimed from the harbour and it is used today for a bowling-green and car parks. Anyone feeding the swans today would be around forty yards further to the left than the girls in the picture. (1375)

The upper view was taken from the northern shore of the Isle of Portland, looking out over the Coaling Pier. Beyond are two Royal Naval Training Ships, *HMS Boscawen* on the right and either *HMS Minotaur* (also known as *Boscawen II*) or *HMS Agincourt* (also known as *Boscawen III*) on the left.

In the right distance is the southern section of the Portland Breakwater, which was completed in 1872. At its end, just behind the masts of *Boscawen*, is the Breakwater Fort. The central section of the breakwater was started in the mid-1890s and finished about a decade later. When this photograph was taken, its future line was marked by a row of 'dolphins' - substantial structures of iron and steel across which nets were stretched to discourage possible raids by small craft, until the permanent breakwaters were constructed. Indistinctly seen in the far distance are the cliffs near Osmington. (1374)

Both of these photographs of Poole Quay were taken from Lower Hamworthy, looking across the Little Channel.

The prominent white building with a portico on the ground floor was the Harbour Office; today it is used by H M Coastguards. To the right, on the other side of the opening of Thames Street onto the Quay, is the medieval building known as the Old Town Cellars, now a museum. To the right of this, with its porticoed doorway partly hidden by masts, is the Customs House which dates from 1788 but which was rebuilt in 1813 after a fire.

The ship on the left of the picture appears to be the *Soridderen*, while that on the right is the *Spirit*. The latter was a 54-foot pilot smack, which had been launched at Poole in 1857. Her first owner was Samuel West Hart, a licensed pilot. In 1889, she was owned by Richard Lovell. She sank at Portland on 15th January 1910, following a collision with a Danish steamer, the *St. Jan*. (823)

James Coventry stood at almost the same spot at the end of Ferry Road to take this shot, looking up the Little Channel to the Poole Bridge, then a wooden structure. Today, it is an opening bridge, the two halves of the roadway rising upwards at approximately two-hourly intervals, to allow shipping access to the West Quay and to the marina in Holes Bay. (824)

Lulworth Cove and Durdle Door, two of the most remarkable geological formations on the south coast, are both part of the Weld family's Lulworth Estate. This extends to 12,000 acres and includes five miles of coastline, as well as the Castle.

This view across the park shows the east front of Lulworth Castle among the trees in the distance. Bowling Green Wood is on the left. James Coventry's sister-in-law Emily (née Weld), was born here and he probably knew Lulworth well from family visits.

The Castle was built of Purbeck Stone in 1608-10 by Thomas Howard. In 1641, the estates were bought by Humphrey Weld, whose wealth originated from his grandfather's success as a London merchant.

The Welds have always been one of Dorset's leading Catholic families. In 1786, they obtained permission from George III to erect the first free-standing Roman Catholic church to be built in England since the Reformation.

The Castle was destroyed by fire in 1929 but the shell has recently been restored by English Heritage and, along with the park and the chapel, is now open to the public. (1221)

Lulworth Cove, seen here from the west. The almost circular cove was formed by erosion of the relatively softer clays and sands, after the sea had broken through the harder limestone rocks to the south. Today it is a major tourist attraction with souvenir shops and tea rooms. Inevitably, most of the many thousands of visitors arrive by car. (1196)

A little over a mile to the west of Lulworth is the huge limestone archway of Durdle Door, always considered a very picturesque spot. The shingle beaches on either side of the headland are reached, either from a car park set back from the cliffs, or more strenuously by way of a section of the Dorset Coast Path from Lulworth. (1186)

The Old Mill Pond at Swanage has been a favourite view for photographers and artists over very many years and the scene has changed little since James Coventry's visit. Today, the steps are partially overgrown by vegetation and it is a lucky photographer who manages to capture this scene without the intrusion of motor vehicles on Church Hill.

     The natural spring which exists in the pond was an important part of the town's water supply for many centuries, but the purity of the water was not improved by the intrusion of cattle and horses wading in to drink! John Mowlem, the great 19th-century benefactor of Swanage and founder of the well-known building firm, put an end to this problem by constructing the wall and steps which we see today. (HRO:25/71)

Three of these four churches are situated in villages on Cranborne Chase. This area of chalk downland, spreading across much of eastern Dorset, was formerly open grassland and a hunting preserve. In the last century much of it became the estate of General Pitt-Rivers, the founder of scientific archaeology. Even today, these villages seem far from the hustle and bustle of modern life.

ABOVE : Pentridge village, which has only one access lane connecting it to the busy Salisbury-Blandford road, nestles into the north-western slopes of Pentridge Hill, a prominent landmark for miles around. The downs in this area bear many tumuli and other evidence for the presence of prehistoric man. Even the village's name is Celtic, derived from 'the hill of the boars'.

St Rumbold's Church was largely rebuilt in Victorian times; its churchyard has recently gained awards from the Dorset Wildlife Trust for its sensitive management. However, the surroundings have changed considerably since Coventry's visit, as the church is screened from this direction, the south-east, by tall sycamore trees and by holly and yew bushes near the porch.

The spot where the girls are posing is now part of the private garden of Orchard House, built in the 1980s. (3966)

LEFT : Gussage All Saints shares the first part of its name with two other villages – Gussage St Andrew and Gussage St Michael. 'Gussage' is derived from the Old English words *gyse* and *sic* meaning gushing stream. The chalk stream concerned, which appears in the foreground of the photograph, is a tributary of the River Allen which joins the Stour at Wimborne Minster.

All Saints Church, which is surprisingly light and spacious inside, dates from the fourteenth century, apart from the chancel which was rebuilt by Ewan Christian in 1864. (4969)

The church of St John the Evangelist, Hinton Martell, is not especially distinguished, having been completely rebuilt in 1870. This followed the demolition of the 13th-century church, which was said at that time to be 'in a state of general decay'.

Prominent in the foreground of the photograph is an ornamental fountain, 'such as may be found ... in front of a gaudy Italian villa', a surprising structure to find in this location! Mr H C Burt was responsible for its construction in about 1870, with the intention of providing drinking water for sheep and other animals. The original decorative centrepiece – the metal one photographed by James Coventry – was replaced by the present one of Portland stone, made by students at a Weymouth college, in 1965. This was unveiled by that year's Miss World, a young lady from Poole. (4961)

At the heart of the Isle of Purbeck, about seven miles to the west of Swanage, is Church Knowle, a largely unspoilt village constructed of the grey local stone.

The photograph shows its parish church, St. Peter's. The trees in the churchyard are less prominent now although this view is obscured by bushes alongside the road. As Knowle is the only village in Purbeck where a priest is mentioned in Domesday Book, this was probably one of the earliest church sites in the district. Most of the present building dates from the thirteenth century. Inside the church is the impressive monumental tomb of John Cavell, a local landowner who died in 1609. Three brasses depict John, his first wife and their four children – and his second wife. (98)

Visit to South-east Hampshire and Sussex

In the summer of 1897, James Coventry made a tour along the south coast as far as Shoreham. For at least part of the way, he was accompanied by his brother, Father Alexander Moray Coventry, who was a priest at Bognor Regis. The numbering of James's negatives, around thirty of them taken on this trip, enables us to follow their route – Portchester, Hayling Island, Warblington, Emsworth, Shoreham (then, sadly, nine negatives are missing) and, on the return journey, Arundel.

This picture of Portchester Castle, taken from inside the outer walls, shows the Landgate.

This was originally a Roman gateway, modified in Norman times and again in the 1390s. The castle was used as a prison in the Napoleonic period, then as a military hospital; these uses came to an end in 1819.

After this, to quote the English Heritage guide book – *'the castle became once more a ruin, increasingly covered with ivy, and a popular place of resort'* – sufficiently so that it was worth someone's while to run 'Tea Gardens' within the ruins at the time of James's and Moray's visit. (1769)

Once again, James took several pictures, either without moving his equipment or after moving it a very short distance. The view of the Landgate and this second view of the Inner Gatehouse with the Keep beyond were taken within a very few feet of one another.

Again we have Father Moray posing, this time against the greenhouse which appears to be connected with the Tea Gardens behind the hedge. The Keep of Portchester Castle is an imposing Norman structure, while the Gatehouse, which always had a drawbridge, was successively extended forwards from the twelfth to the seventeenth centuries. (1771)

An attempt was made in the 1820s to develop the southern shore of Hayling Island into an elegant seaside resort. The Norfolk Crescent, seen behind a lounging Father Coventry, was started in 1825 but never completed. It remains, looking out rather incongruously onto rough grassland and a shingle beach, today fringed with beach huts and ice-cream stands.

  The four white 'pillars' on the left, which are actually just painted mouldings, adorn a house which should have been at the centre of the crescent. While all eight houses to the east of this were completed, including a very grand one at the far end, only one house of the planned western half of the crescent was built. The architect was Robert Adam, commissioned by his *sincere friend*, William Padwick, then the Lord of the Manor. (1772)

On the extreme right of the upper photograph, part of a distant building may be seen – the same one which features more prominently in the lower picture. This was presumably the bathing station, as at least ten bathing machines can be distinguished to the left of it. There is also one on the water's edge, with a winch higher up the beach to pull the machine up again. (1773)

The Church of St Thomas à Becket, Warblington and St James's Church, Emsworth are situated about 1¼ miles apart, near the north-west shore of Chichester Harbour.

Formerly, Warblington was the more important of the two places. As Emsworth grew, in the early middle ages, the inhabitants continued to worship at the ancient parish church, over a mile away across the fields. Although Emsworth had a small brick church of 1789 in the town square, the larger church of St James's was not built until 1840. The combined parish is now known as Warblington-with-Emsworth.

At St Thomas's (above), the eaves come down almost to ground level, with a series of dormer windows set into each slope, giving the church a picturesque appearance. Although much of the church structure dates from the twelfth and thirteenth centuries, parts of the tower show Saxon work and even incorporate re-used Roman tiles. In the churchyard are two small brick and flint huts of about 1800, used by watchmen to prevent night-time grave robbing. (1774)

St James's Church (below) is unusual both inside and out. According to Pevsner and Lloyd in the Hampshire volume of *The Buildings of England*, it has: '… *the weirdest neo-Norman style … west front with attenuated gables … staircases flanking the entrance … vaguely Lombardic colonnades … side-turrets which are decorated with arrow-slits*'.

Unlike Warblington, where the surroundings have changed little since James Coventry's visit, St James's stands in a totally different environment now, much more built up and with far more trees. The boy by the railings is in Church Path where the modern Rectory entrance is now situated. (1778)

Warblington Castle today consists simply of a tall narrow ruin. It has just one turret with an adjoining arch, all that is left of the gatehouse of an early 16th-century moated mansion. This had been built for the Countess of Salisbury - whose empty tomb is in Christchurch Priory. (See page 56.)

The Castle was reduced to a ruin by Parliamentarian forces in 1644, the remaining section being allowed to survive, possibly as a navigational mark. (1775)

Late in the seventeenth or early in the eighteenth century, a house was built within the perimeter of the demolished castle. Many stones from the castle were used in its construction and others have found their way into some 18th-century Emsworth houses.

The modern address of the house is *'Warblington Castle'*. House, ruin, church and cemetery, plus modern farm buildings, are all that is left of the ancient village of Warblington, which still retains the rural setting that James would have seen during his visit in the summer of 1897. (1776)

Arundel Castle has been the home of the Earls of Arundel since the first Earl was created soon after the Norman Conquest. Since 1483, members of the Howard family have also held the title of Duke of Norfolk, still the premier dukedom of the kingdom.

The view in the Quadrangle (above), shows two of the more ancient features still existing at Arundel. On the left is the Barbican, which had a drawbridge on its outer approach and which dates from 1295. Beyond, standing on the earth mound thrown up soon after 1066, is the stone Keep dating from 1138.

      Today the Keep is an open shell, but visitors can climb to the ramparts for a fine view of the surrounding countryside. This picture also shows evidence of the extensive rebuilding which was in progress at the time of James's visit. (1792)

Apart from ancient features like the Keep and Barbican, much of the structure of Arundel Castle to be seen today dates only from the nineteenth century. In the lower picture, taken in the summer of 1897, it is clear that the south-western round tower, visible above the trees towards the left and surmounted by a crane, is still under construction. Nowadays this tower is the highest part visible from this direction, although the tiny trees in the photograph have grown into a great lime avenue which almost blocks this view of the South Front. (1791)

This view of the old Tilting Yard shows the formal garden. An earlier version featured parterres, the outline of which can just be seen on the grass in the foreground. This is the private garden of the Dukes of Norfolk and it seems likely that James and his brother, Father Alexander Moray Coventry, were there at the invitation of Henry, fifteenth Duke of Norfolk, the acknowledged head of the Roman Catholic community in England. (1793)

Dairy Cottage in Mill Road, Arundel, was designed in 1846 by Robert Abraham for the 13th Duke of Norfolk, along with an adjoining octagonal dairy. The cottage is now part of the lease of the Wildfowl and Wetlands Trust; the design of the Visitor Centre there, which won an award for local architect Neil Holland, was inspired by the dairy.

Dairy and Cottage were built on the site of the former Swanbourne Mill, which had been painted, as his last major picture, by John Constable in 1837 – and which was demolished shortly thereafter. Behind the cottage may be seen the bridge, quite new at the time of James's visit, which carries Mill Road over the Mill Stream. Mill Road was laid down by the 15th Duke in 1892 to replace a lane which ran right under the windows of the Castle. (1794)

This is a view of the eastern side of the Slipper Millpond at Emsworth. The large building in the distance is the Slipper Mill, which was built in 1735 and continued milling, using the tidal power of this pond, till the 1940s. The mill itself has since been demolished but the large store house to the east of it still stands, now converted into four private dwellings.

The origin of the 'Slipper' name is probably from Anglo-Saxon *slipor* meaning slippery or *slyppe* meaning slime. The tall chimney on the horizon is all that then remained of the Floodgates Mill. It was built in 1888 but was soon destroyed by fire. The chimney was needed as the mill was designed to work by both water and steam power. The chimney has long been demolished, but was still standing at the time of a 1922 photograph. (1777)

This photograph, taken at Old Shoreham, represents the furthest east that James Coventry is known to have travelled with his camera. It is interesting to note that he included six local children in his shot. St Nicolas's Church has changed little since his visit, but its surroundings have altered almost beyond recognition. Several large pine trees almost block the view of the church from this spot, while the rough track between the fence and the churchyard wall is now the very busy main link from the A27 trunk road to Shoreham town.

The church is a fine structure with a long history. Most of the fabric seen from this direction, the south-west, is of Norman origin, although the western wall is clearly Saxon, with the typical long-and-short work seen on the nearest corner. The tower is a particularly fine example of Norman architecture, supported internally on four beautifully decorated round-headed Norman arches. The tower is very reminiscent of the one at East Meon in Hampshire and both could be by the same architect. (1779)

And finally . . .

Most of James's surviving photographs were taken during the latter years of Queen Victoria's reign. The picture above symbolises the beginning of the Edwardian era.

These Fordingbridge schoolgirls are all dressed in their best clothes to commemorate the Coronation of King Edward VII in the summer of 1902. The planned date for the Coronation was 26th June, but owing to the King's illness it had to be delayed until 9th August. It is probable that this grassy slope is to the south of Parsonage Farm at Fordingbridge, and that the horizontal line below the group of girls is the drive-way into the farm from the south. (4547)

When we started this project, the locations of the photographs were identified only in a list held by the HRO, believed to have been compiled in the 1970s. There were several incorrect guesses which we have been able to correct, while many photographs had no certain location given. Often, we have been able, with the interested help of many people, to pin down locations and to improve the HRO catalogue. (See Appendix, pages 91-94.)

However, some have continued to elude us - including the delightful picture below. The young girl has been set to work rolling the lawn (probably just for the photographic interest) while an adult looks idly on! But whose back lawn is this? - where is this house with its conservatory and arcades?

We hope that someone among our readers will know! (1606)

Locations of James Coventry's photographs in south Wiltshire

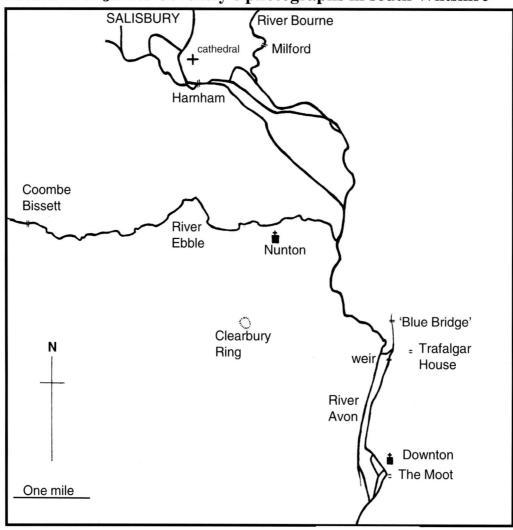

Locations in the Christchurch area

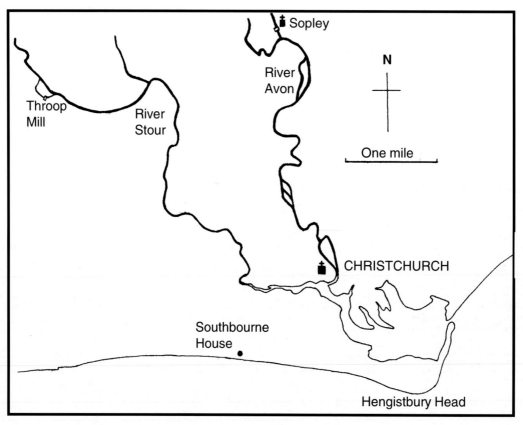

Locations in Dorset

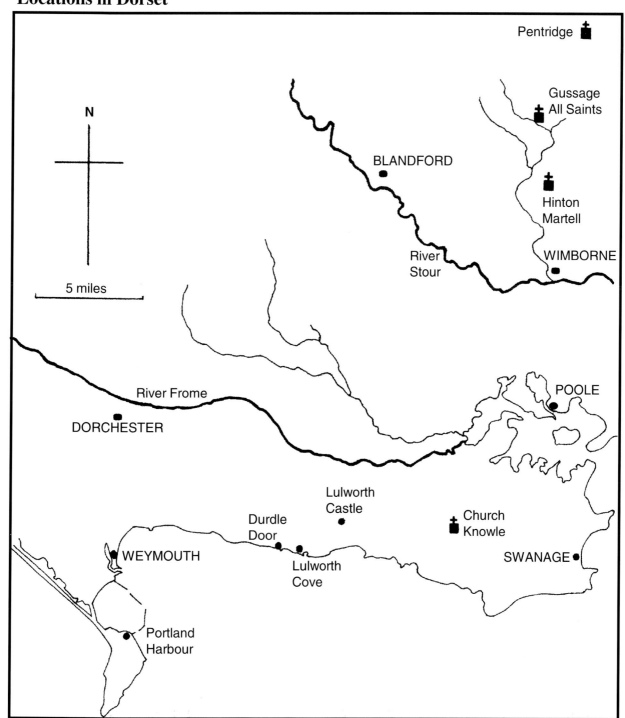

Pentridge

Gussage
All Saints

Hinton
Martell

BLANDFORD

WIMBORNE

River
Stour

N

5 miles

River Frome

DORCHESTER

POOLE

Lulworth
Castle

Durdle
Door

Church
Knowle

WEYMOUTH

Lulworth
Cove

SWANAGE

Portland
Harbour

Locations of photographs taken on the S-E Hampshire and Sussex visit, 1897

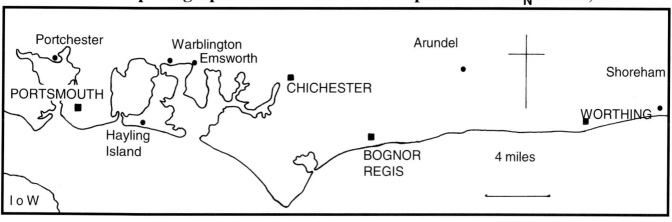

Portchester

Warblington
Emsworth

Arundel

N

Shoreham

PORTSMOUTH

CHICHESTER

WORTHING

Hayling
Island

BOGNOR
REGIS

4 miles

I o W

Simplified Family Tree of the Coventry Family of Burgate House, Fordingbridge

1. John, 1793-1870 (m. 1818, Elizabeth Wilson, d. 1856; m. Louisa Rollestone, d.1857; m. Ellen Wyndham Penruddock, d. 1905)

  2. John, 1819-97 (m. 1842, Catherine Seton, 1818-1901)

    3a. Margaret Elizabeth, 1843-94 (unmarried)

    3b. **John, 1845-1933** (m. 1856, Emily Weld)

      4a. Mary Flora, 1877-? (unmarried)

      4b. Constance Catherine Mary, 1879-1961 (nun)

      4c. Philomena Barbara Mary, 1880-? (nun)

      4d. **John Joseph, 1882-1950** (m. 1910, Margaret Camilla Macartney)

        5a. Five daughters

      4e. Annette Emily Mary, 1884-? (m. 1907, Maj-Gen Sir Philip Gordon Grant)

        5b. One son

      4f. Bernard Seton, 1887-? (m. 1910, Anne Cunningham)

        5c. Two sons

      4g. William St John, 1893-1914 (killed in action)

    3c. Florence Catherine, 1846-1936 (unmarried)

    3d. JAMES SETON, 1849-1917 (unmarried)

    3e. Walter Bulkeley, 1850-? (unmarried)

    3f. Marion, 1851-1934 (nun)

    3g. Alexander Moray, 1853-1925 (priest)

    3h. Isabella Anne, 1854-1936 (nun)

    3i. Barbara, 1856-1946 (nun)

    3j. Bernard, 1859-1929 (m. Ella Gordon Dalgeish)

      4h. Muriel Mary, 1895-? (unmarried)

      4i. Catherine Mary Aline, 1898-? (m. Lt-Col Frederick Munn)

        5d. One son and two daughters

      4j. Bernadine Mary Joan, 1903-? (unmarried)

      4k. Isabella Mary, 1905-? (unmarried)

    3k. Gertrude Mary Philomena, 1862-1955 (m. Henry Radcliffe)

      4l. * Gertrude Mary Katherine, b.1903 (m. Philip George Bower)

      4m. Henry Edward Joseph, b. 1904

    3l. Francis Martin, 1863-1917 (m. Amy Maud Hill)

      4n. Gerald Leslie, 1900-?

      4o. Catherine Nora, b.1906 (m. Hubert de Burgh Williams)

        5e. Two sons

KEY :

1. James's grand-parents

  2. James's parents

    3. James's brothers and sisters

      4. James's nephews and nieces

        5. James's grand-nephews and grand nieces

This family tree is provided to clarify some of the relationships mentioned in the Introduction and in the captions to the family photographs. We make no claim that it is complete and apologise for any possible errors.

Those names shown in **bold** were the owners of Burgate House in each generation.

* Mrs Bower was our main family contact, who assisted in identifying family members in several photographs.

Appendix – a catalogue of James Coventry's negatives

Column 1 : consecutive negative number as inscribed on the edge of each glass plate.
Column 2 : number of wooden box in which the negatives are stored at the HRO.
Column 3 : within each box, the number of the slot which holds the negative. (The correct HRO reference number for each negative is **33M84/box no./slot no.**)
Column 4 : the HRO reference number of prints prepared by Philip Allison. (Add the prefix **105M93/** before each code listed to give the full reference number.)
Column 5 : the page number on which the photograph appears in this book.
Column 6 : the photograph number for those which appeared in *Fordingbridge and District – a Pictorial History* by the present authors (Phillimore 1994).
Column 7 : the page number on which the photograph appeared in Philip Allison's *The New Forest – a photographic record of 100 years of Forest Life* (Pioneer Publications 1979).
Column 8 : a brief description of the content of the photograph.
Column 9 : dates, estimated as described on page 16.

1	2	3	4	5	6	7	8	9
0034	11	01		29			Boating on the River	
0098	11	02		79			Church at Church Knowle, Dorset	
0133	11	03		18	162		Donkey cart outside Burgate House	
0501	11	05					Big oak in parkland - New Forest	
0509	11	04					Eyeworth - pond and wood beyond	Summer 1892 or 93
0526	11	06					Wooded river banks	
0533	11	07		61			Romsey Abbey	
0537	11	08					Furzehill - Dorridge Hill	
0694	11	09	5/08	49			Eel trap in Avon	
0780	11	10		6	158		James Coventry - the photographer	Summer 1893
0781	----	----	6/77	23			Aunt E and girls	
0823	11	11		75			Poole Customs House Quay	
0824	11	12		75			View up the channel to Poole Bridge	
0873	11	13					Avon Valley and River from Godshill	
0875	11	14		56			Christchurch Priory	
0876	11	15		70			Salisbury Cathedral & R Avon	
0877	11	16					Salisbury Cathedral & R Avon	
0907	----	----	3/48				Pitts Wood	
0918	11	17		63			Somerley - Ringwood Lodge	
0921	11	18		27	1		Church Square, Fordingbridge	
0922	11	19					Church Square, Fordingbridge	
0949	11	20					Flood from Burgate	November 1894
0952	11	50					Flooded water meadows	
0954	11	21		46			Flood, with haystack, from Burgate	
0955	11	22		46			Flood from Burgate	
0956	11	23		47			Flooded river with tree	
1034	11	24					Downland view with Clearbury Ring	
1063	----	----	5/44	68			The Tannery, Downton	Summer 1895
1065	11	25		68			Downton Moot	
1066	11	26					Avon at Downton with hatches	
1067	11	27		68			Downton from the Moot	
1068	11	28		67			Footbridge and weir, Trafalgar	
1070	11	29					River Avon, Trafalgar Ho. in distance	
1071	11	30	3/26,5/55	67			Blue Bridge, Trafalgar	
1073	11	31	6/38				Avon Shallows, below Breamore Mill	
1078	11	32					The Avon at Longford	
1079	11	33		69			Clearbury Ring, near Downton	
1084	11	34					Road in Inclosures - Woodgreen-Godshill	
1115	11	35		43			Cattle in Latchmore Brook	
1117	11	36					Old oak, High Corner, near Nice's Farm	
1118	11	37					Old oak, High Corner, near Nice's Farm	
1119	11	38					Pitts Wood	
1120	11	39					Pitts Wood	
1121	11	40					Pitts Wood	
1122	11	41					Pitts Wood	
1123	11	42					Pitts Wood	
1124	11	43					Ashley Lodge Gate - Pitts Wood Inclosure	
1128	11	44					Road through Godshill Inclosure	
1129	11	45					Godshill Wood	
1130	11	46		45			Godshill Wood	
1135	11	52		63			Somerley House - terraces	
1186	11	47		77			Durdle Door, Lulworth	
1196	11	48		76			Lulworth Cove	
1221	11	51	5/48	76			Lulworth Castle	
1261	11	53		53	164	65	Lady A Goff in a gig nr Hale Church	Winter 1895/96
1276	11	54		65			Teffont Evias Park, House & Church	
1282	11	55					Chalk downland (Knowle Hill, Bowerchalke)	
1283	11	56					As 1282, with shepherd's hut	
1284	11	57					As 1282 and 1283, different angle	

1	2	3	2	5	6	7	8	9
1285	11	58					Vereley Wood, near Burley	Winter 1895/96
1286	11	59					Vereley Wood, near Burley	
1287	11	60					Vereley Wood, near Burley	
1288	11	61					Vereley Wood, near Burley	
1289	11	62					Old beech pollards, (Burley?)	
1290	11	63					Old beech pollards, (Burley?)	
1291	11	64		45			Old beech trees, Ridley Wood, Burley	
1292	11	65					Old beech pollards, Ridley Wood, Burley	
1293	11	66					Old beech pollards, Burley	
1294	11	67					Old beech pollards, Vereley Wood, Burley	
1295	11	68					Vereley Wood, Burley	
1296	11	69					Vereley Wood, Burley	
1297	11	70					Old beech pollards (Burley)	
1298	11	71					Old beech pollards, Burley	
1300	11	72					Ride through old beech pollards (Burley?)	
1301	11	73					Old planted oak, (Burley?)	
1302	11	74					Fallen beech tree, (Burley?)	
1303	11	75					Beech pollards, three in line, (Burley?)	
1304	11	76					Beech pollards, (Burley?)	
1305	11	77					Ridley Wood, Burley	
1306	11	78					Pitts Wood, near Fordingbridge	
1307	11	79					Old beech trees	
1308	11	80					Old beech trees	
1323	11	81					Edge of old wood	
1324	11	82					Beech pollards, Bratley Wood, Boldrewood	
1330	11	83					Fryern Court, Fordingbridge, with wisteria	
1348	11	84	6/157	71			Carriage outside Arundells, Salisbury Close	
1350	11	85	3/28	72			Milford Bridge, Salisbury	
1352	11	86					Forest ride through conifers	
1353	11	87		72			Figures by river	
1355	11	88	5/154,6/35	73			Harnham Bridge, 2 girls on river bank	
1356	11	89	6/155	71			Garden of North Canonry, Salisbury	Summer 1896
1374	11	90		74			Coaling Pier with ships, Portland	
1375	11	91		74			Weymouth Harbour, swans and girls	
1403	16	01	1/20	12		76	King and Queen Oaks, Boldrewood	
1405	16	02		17	159		Burgate House with figures	
1436			6/14	26	16		Old Court House, Fordingbridge	
1444	16	03		28	13		Horseport, Fordingbridge	
1445	16	04					Horseport, Fordingbridge	
1458	16	05		28			Rowing near Bridge House, Fordingbridge	
1460	16	06					River and boathouse, Burgate	
1462	16	07			15		Court House from Burgate South Lodge	
1465	16	08					Wooded river bank	
1468	16	09		60			Romsey Abbey, from Church Place	
1475	16	10					River with wooded banks, rowboat	
1476	16	11		29	107		Cleric rowing below Fordingbridge bridge	
1477	16	12		26			Fordingbridge church from meadows	
1490	16	13					Sunken green lane	
1492	16	14		52			Girl at hatches in woods (Burgate?)	Winter 1896/97
1493	16	15					Girl at hatches in woods (Burgate?)	
1497	16	16					R Avon nr Burgate House, with boathouse	
1499	16	17					May Coventry & birdcage at Burgate House	
1500	16	18		20			May C. reading, at Burgate House	
1505	16	19		17	31		North Lodge, Burgate, girl at the gate	
1512	16	20		40			Avonside, Criddlestyle; figures in garden	
1513	16	21					Avonside, different view, horse in foreground	
1525	16	22					'Battlefield Church', Shrewsbury – title inscribed on purchased (?) negative	
1541	16	23					Lane with house beyond, location unknown	
1542	16	24					Trees reflected in pond	
1575	16	25		47			Gale-damaged tree and cow	
1580	16	26		33	56		Breamore Churchyard with girls	
1581	16	27			26		Well Cottage, Breamore, with two girls	
1582	16	28			25		Yewtree Farm, Breamore (destroyed by fire 1995)	
1584	16	29					Trees in flooded hollow (Fry's Hill, Breamore?)	
1585	16	30		57			Southbourne House, now demolished	
1590	16	31		57			Low sea cliffs at Hengistbury Head	
1596	16	32					Path through woods with child	
1598	16	33		40			Two horsemen and girl - Criddlestyle	
1602	16	34					Large thatched house, location unknown	
1606	16	35					Child on lawn of large house, location unknown	
1609	16	36		20			Three Coventry children in fancy dress	
1614	16	37		20			Clown costume, John Joseph Coventry	
1624	16	38					Lane and brick wall (North End, Harbridge?)	
1626	16	39		33			Rockbourne Church	
1632	16	40			34		Bicton Mill from downstream	

1	2	3	4	5	6	7	8	9
1634	16	41	5/40	48			Bicton Farm house from across the Avon	
1635	16	42					Bicton village street with three girls	
1638	16	43					Meadow, (Priory Meadow, Breamore?)	
1648	16	44		64			Four children on wall at Breamore House	
1650	16	45	6/08	51			Gorley School	Spring 1897
1663	16	46			17		Burgate South Lodge from inside grounds	
1668	25	env	5/05	42			Thatched cottages, South Gorley	Summer 1897
1673	16	47		21			Girls in straw hats playing Aunt Sally	
1674	16	48		21	161		Girls playing ring-a-ring o'roses	
1682	16	49					Fordingbridge Town Hall	
1683	16	50		9			Fordingbridge church from graveyard	
1691	16	51					View of Fordingbridge from west of Avon	
1692	16	52					View of Fordingbridge from west of Avon	
1693	16	53		36	29		Outwick village, children in donkey cart	
1694	16	54					Conifers in park	
1695	16	55					Road through trees	
1696	16	56		51	46		Harbridge School, Somerley	
1697	16	57		38			Cottage at Harbridge (same cottage in 1750)	
1709	16	100					Group of 8 women and 3 men	
1710	16	58		19	160		Group of 8 women and 3 men	
1724	16	59		53			Moyles Court from meadows	
1725	16	60					Moyles Court - rear view	
1726	16	61		53			The ford at Moyles Court	
1727	16	62	1/22	53		27	Moyles Court Oak, ford beyond	
1728	16	63					New Forest stream through woodland	
1729	16	64					New Forest stream through woodland	
1734	16	65					Cottage (Whitsbury Road, Fordingbridge?)	
1739	25	env		48		81	Bicton Mill from upstream	
1742	16	66					Cottage near Burgate Cross	
1743	16	67	5/53				Lilac Cottage, Burgate	
1744	16	68			18		Blissford Hill, one figure	
1745	16	69		41		118	Blissford Hill, bottom, 2 men and 3 girls	
1746	16	70	5/36	42			Millersford Bottom and Godshill Inclosure	
1747	16	71	6/07				Brook and barn (Upper Millersford?)	
1748	16	72					Millersford Brook, Arden Cottage	
1749	16	73					Burgate House from the park	
1750	16	74		38			Cottage at Harbridge; children in foreground	
1751	16	75					Hamer Bridge, Somerley, children in stream	
1752	16	76	5/37	52			Hamer Bridge, Somerley, children in stream	
1755	16	77	6/06				Blissford Ford and Newmans Cottage	
1757	16	78	5/54				Burgate Manor House	
1768	16	79					General view of Portchester Castle	
1769	16	80		80			Gateway of Portchester Castle	
1770	16	81					The Keep, Portchester Castle	
1771	16	82		80			Entrance with figure, Portchester Castle	
1772	16	83		81			Norfolk Crescent from the beach, Hayling Island	
1773	16	84		81			Beach, Hayling Island	
1774	16	85		82			St Thomas à Becket, Warblington	
1775	16	86		83			Warblington Castle	
1776	16	87		83			House adjoining Warblington Castle	
1777	16	88	5/06	86			Children on beach of Slipper Millpond, Emsworth	
1778	16	89		82			St James's Church, Emsworth	
1779	16	90		86			St Nicolas's Church, Old Shoreham	
1789	16	91					Arundel Castle – S facade under construction	
1791	16	92		84			Arundel Castle – S facade under construction	
1792	16	93		84			Arundel Castle - ancient keep and barbican	
1793	16	94		85			Tilting Yard, Arundel Castle	
1794	16	95		85			Dairy Cottage at Arundel	
1795	16	96					Swanbourne Lake, Arundel	
1797	16	97					Swanbourne Lake, Arundel	
1809	16	98		32	39		Rockbourne village street with children	
1814	16	99	3/43	78			Stonehenge	
1815	25	01					Stonehenge, children lying on grass in foreground	
1817	25	env		41			Winnie Bush's Cottage, Frogham	
1873	----	----	6/11				Winnie Bush's Cottage, Frogham	
1891	25	02		30	9		Fordingbridge Town Hall	
1951	25	03		17			Young girl in a greenhouse	Autumn 1897
1956	25	04					Woodland stream	
1969	25	05	5/35	55			Sopley church, children in foreground	Winter 1897/98
1970	25	06	5/34	55			Sopley church and mill, flooded river	
1971	25	07		51			Harbridge church from water meadows	
1986	25	08		54			West Street, Ringwood from the river	
2022	25	09					Large house by river, location unknown	
2036	25	76		36	Fr'p'ce		Cottage and vegetable garden (Outwick)	
2037	25	10	5/02				Village street with children (location unknown)	
2042	25	11					Road alongside inclosure fence, girl by tree	

1	2	3	4	5	6	7	8	9
2071	25	12	5/22,6/27	42			Hasley Inclosure from Hyde Common	Summer 1898
2175	25	13					Avon from Burgate House	
2177	25	14		34	28		Boy in Breamore Stocks	
2197	25	15					Breamore Church from SE	
2230	25	77		7			Farmyard with figures (location uncertain)	
2234	25	78		35			Same farmyard, outbuildings	
2256	25	16					Burgate House, water meadows in foreground	
2257	25	17		31	41		Mill End, Damerham, with figures	Winter 1898/99
2264	25	79		31	40		South End, Damerham	
2266	25	80		37			Cottage garden with 3 figures, location unknown	
2278	25	18					Beech pollards with three girls	
2280	25	19					Ride through hardwood, 2 girls on log	
2281	25	20					Similar to 25/19, girls standing	
2310	25	21					Sheep on downland, Ducks Nest, Rockbourne	
2311	25	22		35			Sheep on downland with three pine trees	
2313	25	23					Girl at foot of large pollard	
2314	25	24		64			Lime avenue, Breamore House grounds	
2319	25	25		54			Bridge between Ringwood and Ashley Heath	
2321	25	26		39			Cottage, 7 children on a gate, location unknown	
2328	25	27					Court Farm, Damerham	
2329	25	28		34			Court Farm, Damerham	
2345	25	81		32	38		Rockbourne village street with figures	
2424	25	29		71			Salisbury Cathedral, West Front	Summer 1899
2437	25	30		41	20		Hannington, top of Penton's Hill, Frogham	
2465	25	31		62			West Park, Rockbourne, gateway with lodges	
2481	25	32			45		Figures in lane, College House, Martin	
2493	25	33	prob.3/33	50			Ibsley Bridge	
2494	25	34	5/50	50			Hatches below Ibsley Bridge	
2495	25	35	5/49				Hatches below Ibsley Bridge	
2517	25	36		23		120	Two girls in a water meadow (Burgate?)	
2523	25	37		22			Rustic bridge, Burgate	
2535	25	38					3 children by drive entrance, location unknown	
2546	25	39					Trafalgar House, recumbent man	
2548	25	40		66			Trafalgar House, recumbent man	
2564	25	82	1/10	43			Footbridge over Hucklesbrook, Furze Hill	
2572	25	41					Girl by river (at Burgate?)	
2576	25	83		39			Girl with pram by cottage, location unknown	
2583	25	42					Small side door of church	
2585	25	43					Boy by church window and slab tomb	
2591	25	44					Chapter House of Salisbury Cathedral	
3040*	----	----	5/26	19			2 girls and donkey	
3040*	----	----	3/61	58			11 children paddling at beach	
3531	25	45					Cliff scenery, probably Dorset	
3882	25	46					Cliff scenery, probably Dorset	
3883	25	47					Cliff scenery, probably Dorset	
3884	25	48					Cliff scenery, probably Dorset	
3885	25	49					Cliff scenery, probably Dorset	
3942	25	51	2/22	44		105	The Butt Fritham, round barrow	
3964	25	52	2/21	44		117	Nomansland, 2 girls in foreground	
3966	25	53		78			Pentridge Church, 3 girls in foreground	
4101	25	54					River scene, location unknown	
4540	25	55		56			Throop Mill, outskirts of Bournemouth	
4547	25	84		87			Girls celebrating coronation of Ed. VII	August 1902
4946	25	56					Graves of John and Catherine Coventry	
4948	25	57					Longleat	
4949	25	58		66			Longleat	
4953	25	59	6/156	69			Nunton Church, children in foreground	
4961	25	60	5/04	79			Hinton Martell village street and church	
4969	25	61		78			Gussage All Saints Church	
4977	25	62		59			Arch Rock, Freshwater Bay (collapsed 1992)	
4984	25	63		59			Children on beach, Freshwater Bay	
5004	25	64					Wooded river banks	
5071	25	65		73			Hump-backed bridge at Coombe Bissett	
5624	25	66					Steep wooded river bank (Sandy Balls, Godshill)	
---	25	67					Woman on river bank	DATING NOT POSSIBLE
---	25	68		27			Provost Street, Fordingbridge	
---	25	69		60			Romsey Abbey from North	
---	25	70		61			Saxon Rood and Abbesses Doorway, Romsey Abbey	
---	25	71	5/52	77			Old Mill Pond, Swanage	
---	25	72					River, ruins on opposite bank (location unknown)	
---	25	73					River with weir, rocky cliff to left (location unknown)	
---	25	74					Wide river or pool, haystack (location unknown)	
	11	49					No negative in slot 11 / 49	
	25	50					No negative in slot 25 / 50	
	25	75					No negative in slot 25 / 75	

*According to notes on the back of P. Allison's prints, both of these photos were from a negative numbered 3040!

Index

Sources and acknowledgements

The majority of the photographs in this book are held as glass negatives in the Hampshire Record Office, Winchester, which also holds copyright. Those photographs enclosed within boxes, bearing a 'PA' reference at the end of the caption, are held by the HRO as prints in the Phillip Allison collection. The HRO reference number of any picture in this book may be determined by reference to the Appendix.

Our sincere thanks for their co-operation and interest, over a period of some years, go to the County Archivist and the staff of the HRO, especially Linda Champ and Sarah Lewin. Trevor Evans, a photographer with the Hampshire Museums Service, made most of the modern prints from the glass negatives, enabling this project to go ahead. Our thanks also to Mrs Allison of Frogham who first loaned us some James Coventry prints from her late husband's collection.

Boxed photographs without a PA reference have been copied from the one Coventry family album still known to be in existence. This is part of the John Shering Collection, the nucleus, it is to be hoped, of a future Fordingbridge Museum; our thanks to John for permission to make these copies.

James's print of the cottage at North Gorley, seen on page 37, is in private hands and came to our attention almost by chance; many thanks to Mrs A Crouter of Gorley for loaning, and allowing us to copy, this treasured family relic.

Six illustrations used in the Introduction, not James Coventry photographs, came from other sources. On page 13, the photograph of Catherine Coventry was copied from a locket loaned to us by Mrs Gertrude Bower; while the portraits of J J Coventry and his wife were copied from original oils held by The Game Conservancy – our thanks to Peter Lambson, Judy Pittock and Charles Nodder. On page 14, James Coventry's tombstone was photographed by Gerald Ponting; while the Zouave picture was down-loaded from the Internet and used with the permission of Yvon Martin (Archives nationales du Québec) and Jean-Louis Parent (l'Association des zouaves pontificaux de Trois-Rivières). The Instantograph advertisement on page 15 was provided by Colin Harding of the National Museum of Photography in Bradford (who also checked the photography section of the Introduction).

Information for the Introduction came from many sources and the compilation of a detailed bibliography would be impossible. Again, the Coventry family archives in the HRO (refs. 8M59 and 212M87) have been invaluable, as has the information in Debrett's Peerage. James Coventry's will was obtained from the Probate Office in York. The Portsmouth Catholic Diocesan Archivist provided valuable information on the history of Fordingbridge Catholic Church and Mr & Mrs Devario Matteucci of Chandler's Ford kindly translated one of the Servite Fathers' documents from the Italian. Record Offices in Caernarfon and Devon filled in small parts of the family history; as did reference to copies of the *Salisbury and Winchester Journal* (1840-1917) held on microfilm by the Salisbury Local Studies Library.

Information on James Coventry's service with the Pontifical Zouaves was provided by Denis Roy of Bibliothèque Nationale du Québec, Montréal, after we had obtained a reference from an archivist at The Vatican. Other Zouave information came mainly from a variety of web-sites.

The proprietor of Arundel Photographica gave us our earliest information about the Lancaster Instantograph, later extended by Rob Neiderman (by e-mail from Minnesota) and by Bill Phillips of the Hampshire Museums Service. A number of books on early photography proved useful, notably Robert White's *Discovering Old Cameras 1839-1939*, (Shire, 1995); Robert Pols's *Dating Old Photographs* (Federation of Family History Societies, 1992); and John Hannavy's *Victorian Photographers at Work* (Shire, 1997).

Many people assisted us in tracking down the locations of some of the photographs. Roger Guttridge, in the Bournemouth *Evening Echo*, and Peter Daniels, in the *Salisbury Journal*, each ran features on one or more of the 'mystery photographs'. It would be impossible to list all those who perused the old pictures, either in the papers or at meetings, and offered their opinions on locations; but Robert Drew, John Upton and Patricia James need special mention as providing positive identifications of previously unknown views.

Much of the information in the captions came from a wide variety of guide-books, English Heritage handbooks, church history leaflets and the like. The *Hampshire and Isle of Wight* volume in *The Buildings of England* series by Nikolaus Pevsner and David Lloyd was regularly consulted. Invaluable local information was provided by Maureen Attwooll of Weymouth Library; Sara Rodger, Assistant Librarian at Arundel Castle; David Julian of the Wildfowl and Wetlands Trust, Arundel; staff of the Portsmouth Record Office; Canon David Partridge, the Vicar of Emsworth; Strahan Soames and Dorothy Bone of the Emsworth Maritime and Historical Trust; Lindsay Burtenshaw, Agent, Somerley Estate; Dai Watkins of Poole Museums Service; Bill Wintrip and Margaret Collins of Lulworth. Major Nigel Chamberlayne-Macdonald of Cranbury Park gave us the benefit of his expert knowledge of horse-drawn carriages. Barbara Hillier and Bernard Hawton both assisted with proof-reading.

Jill Wilkinson and Ron Smith of the Julia Margaret Cameron Trust, Dimbola Lodge, Isle of Wight have taken great interest in the project and provided a venue for our book launch and for the first public exhibition of a small selection of James Coventry prints.

Our thanks must go to members of the Coventry family who have supported our project. John Coventry of Bodmin put us in touch with Mrs Gertrude Bower, James Coventry's one surviving niece. A visit to her home near Bridgwater, and subsequent long telephone conversations, proved one of the highlights of the research for this book. We cannot thank her enough for her interest and information – and her friendship.

Our wives, Elizabeth Light and Elizabeth Ponting, have helped in many ways, not least in joining us on visits to the spots where James took his photographs – and taking part in the wild-goose-chases which this sometimes involved !

Finally, our grateful thanks to all those many unnamed people who have taken an interest in our research in some way or another - and our sincere apologies for any errors which may remain in our text.